THE ULTIMATE INSTANT POT
DESSERTS COOKBOOK

THE ULTIMATE INSTANT POT DESSERTS COOKBOOK

EASY RECIPES FOR CAKES, PIES, AND DECADENT BREAKFAST TREATS

JANET A. ZIMMERMAN

COVER PHOTOGRAPHY BY DARREN MUIR

ROCKRIDGE
PRESS

Interior and Cover Designer: Carlos Esparza
Art Producer: Janice Ackerman
Editor: Rebecca Markley
Production Editor: Andrew Yackira
Production Manager: Martin Worthington

Cover Photography © 2021 Darren Muir; food styling by Yolanda Muir. Interior Photography ii: © Evi Abeler; vi: ©Darren Muir; viii-ix: ©Marija Vidal; x: ©Darren Muir; p. 14: ©Shea Evans; p. 26: ©Hélène Dujardin; p. 28: ©Marija Vidal; p. 32: ©Hélène Dujardin; p. 36: ©Jennifer Martine; p. 50: ©Laura Flippen; p. 58: ©Nadine Greeff; p. 68: ©Iain Bagwell; p. 72: ©Nadine Greeff; p. 78: ©Annie Martin; p. 82: ©Marija Vidal; p. 92: ©Trent Lanz/Stocksy; p. 94: ©Darren Muir. Author photo courtesy of Mast Photography.

Paperback ISBN: 978-1-63878-204-9
eBook ISBN: 978-1-63878-506-4

R0

To Dave, who always makes it all work out.

CHOCOLATE-CARAMEL SAUCE, PAGE 86

CONTENTS

INTRODUCTION

When I was growing up, our family dinners almost always ended with dessert, partly because that's just what homemakers did back then and partly because my dad had a sweet tooth. So my mother made sure to serve us a slice of pie or cake or even just cookies and ice cream.

But even though I was used to ending the meal with something rich and sweet, when I moved out I rarely made my own desserts. It wasn't that I didn't like them. Desserts just seemed like way too much work.

As I gained cooking experience and began my career as a food writer and recipe developer, I still shied away from making desserts. (I had no trouble eating them!) I made do with a few of my mother's standbys and a couple of easy no-bake recipes, but I concentrated my work on savory dishes.

Long before electric pressure cookers and multicookers like the Instant Pot were available, I was using a stove-top pressure cooker to speed up all kinds of savory dishes, from risotto to short ribs to pinto beans. Yet it never occurred to me to use it for desserts until I wrote my first pressure cooker cookbook. I had to include a chapter on desserts, and necessity (or pressure, no pun intended) being the mother of invention, I discovered a world of sweet treats that could be cooked in the appliance.

The first recipe I tried was for individual cheesecakes. I'd tried making cheesecake the traditional way but never with much success. Imagine my

surprise when my little cheesecake gems came out beautifully. Easy, quick, and delicious—everything I wanted in a dessert recipe.

It turns out that the steamy environment of the Instant Pot is perfect for producing not only light and creamy cheesecakes but also perfectly smooth custards and rustic bread puddings. I started with those and then moved on to more challenging recipes. Because you can't get any browning in a pressure cooker, cookies and crisp pastries won't work, but it turns out that with the right ingredients and timing, you can make delicious pound cakes, brownies, muffins, and lava cakes.

Since that first book, I've become a big fan of Instant Pot desserts. This book contains some classic recipes, some international specialties, and some new twists on old favorites. Along with my new creations, I've included some favorites from my previous books and some contributions from other experienced cookbook authors.

Whether you're looking for elegant desserts suitable for company, treats for the kids' after-school snacks, a sweet addition to brunch, or an easy finale to date night, you'll find recipes to meet all your needs, whatever your tastes and skill level.

I hope you like cooking from this book as much as I liked writing it and that you, too, will fully embrace the world of Instant Pot desserts.

PEACH AND BLUEBERRY COBBLER, PAGE 54

CHAPTER 1

WHIPPING UP DESSERTS IN YOUR INSTANT POT

Welcome to the world of Instant Pot desserts. Before we get to the recipes, it's helpful to take a look at the Instant Pot itself and how it works. In this chapter you'll learn cooking techniques and tips that will ensure great results every time. Specifically, this chapter will cover equipment and ingredients, which types of desserts work best in a pressure cooker, how to use the Instant Pot, and how to avoid common pitfalls.

A NEW WAY TO MAKE YOUR FAVORITE DESSERTS

Over the past few years, the Instant Pot has transformed the way many home cooks make dinner. But while many people have come to rely on this innovative appliance for entrées and side dishes such as braised short ribs and lentil soup, fewer know how fantastic an Instant Pot can be when it comes to desserts.

Now, it's true that you can't bake crisp cookies, fluffy chiffon-style cakes, or flaky pastries in an Instant Pot. But you can make incomparably smooth cheesecakes, silky custards, and creamy puddings; luscious pound cakes and Bundt cakes; and quick fruit desserts and irresistible sauces. With so many options, you might never go back to the oven for dessert.

If you bake desserts in your oven, you're probably used to peeking through the window to check on the progress, removing pans to change their position, and testing frequently to gauge when your dessert is done. You may at first feel insecure without those tricks, but the Instant Pot's reliability and precision will soon win you over.

And you're not relearning how to bake here. With the Instant Pot, you may be using a different cooking method—pressure cooking—but the ingredients and preparation are remarkably similar to those in conventionally baked desserts. It's time to dive into some of the main cooking techniques used with the Instant Pot.

Five Reasons to Make Dessert in the Instant Pot

Need a little more convincing that the Instant Pot is dessert's best friend? Here are just five of the many advantages you'll experience.

A SUMMERTIME DREAM. When the weather is warm, you can cook a delectable dessert without turning on the oven, keeping yourself cool. You'll save energy, too.

HANDS-OFF, WORRY-FREE DESSERTS. Once your dessert is in the Instant Pot, you can lock on the lid and walk away, knowing that you'll have a perfect sweet treat when time is up.

QUICKER COOK TIMES. Pressure cooking can cut cooking time by as much as half, so you'll get dessert on the table sooner.

THE ULTIMATE HOLIDAY HELPER. On holidays, when the oven is working overtime and burner space is at a premium, you can still whip up dessert using the Instant Pot while you concentrate on the rest of the meal.

EASY START, EASY FINISH. The recipes in this book involve minimal prep and easy cleanup. In most cases, you won't even have to clean the Instant Pot after use.

MAIN COOKING TECHNIQUES

The Instant Pot is a true multicooker, with functions for pressure cooking, slow cooking, yogurt making, sautéing, and rice cooking. (Some models have extra functions, such as sous vide cooking.) Almost all the recipes in this book use the Pressure Cook function, either cooking right in the inner pot or steaming on the trivet; a few also use the Sauté function.

SIMMERING, SAUTÉING, AND BROWNING

Using the Sauté function, you can sear meats, sauté vegetables, deglaze, or simmer sauces just as easily as on the stove top. For dessert recipes, the feature is used primarily for cooking pie filling (Brandy-Soaked Cherry Cheater Pie, page 57), melting or browning butter (Browned-Butter Apple Spice Cake, page 16), or reducing sauces after cooking (White Wine–Poached Pears with Vanilla, page 59).

PRESSURE COOKING

Pressure cooking is the main technique used in this book's recipes. Simply put, pressure cooking is cooking with liquid in a sealed pot. As the liquid comes to a boil, steam is trapped inside, raising the pressure in the pot.

And as the pressure rises, so too does the boiling point of the liquid, further increasing the pressure. This means that foods cook faster than with conventional methods. Some of the recipes in this book call for cooking a dessert right in the pot, such as Coconut-Almond Rice Pudding (page 77) and Peach Dumplings (page 56), but more frequently, the dessert is assembled in a baking dish or dishes, placed on the trivet, and pressure steamed (see the following section).

STEAMING

The Instant Pot steams food under pressure, maintaining a precise temperature throughout the steaming process. Steaming is the best method for creating silky puddings and perfectly creamy cheesecakes, such as Chocolate Cookie Cheesecake (page 34). Steaming will also produce smooth custard sauces, such as Lemon Curd (page 85), without the constant stirring necessary on the stove top. Do not confuse pressure steaming with the Steam function, which is typically used for things like steaming vegetables and does not apply to any of the recipes in this book.

GETTING TO KNOW THE POT

If you're new to the Instant Pot, it can look intimidating, but it's easy to use with a little practice. Here's a primer on the parts and control panel.

PARTS

The parts of the Instant Pot are a bit different from traditional pots and pans. If you're familiar with other pressure cookers, you'll recognize most of these.

THE BASE contains the heating element, which is completely enclosed. The outside of the base is where you'll find the control panel.

THE CONTROL PANEL varies from model to model. It can be a touch screen, a dial, buttons, or a combination. You'll use it to choose the cooking function, set the pressure level and time, and cancel cooking when done (in some models).

THE LID is designed to lock into place and seal completely so that the unit can cook under pressure. It contains a sealing ring, steam release handle, and float valve.

THE SEALING RING is made of silicone and fits securely under the edge of the lid. Before securing the lid, make sure it's seated correctly and doesn't have any nicks or tears.

THE STEAM RELEASE HANDLE is used to release the pressure after cooking. In some models, it has to be moved from "sealing" to "venting"; in others, the default position is "sealing" and pressure is released by pressing a button on the handle.

THE FLOAT VALVE is a pin-lock mechanism that rises upon reaching pressure and falls when pressure is released. It keeps the lid from opening while the unit is under pressure.

THE INNER POT is a removable stainless steel or nonstick pot where the actual cooking occurs, whether directly in the pot or on a trivet over water.

CONTROLS

The control panel on the Instant Pot includes selections for all the main cooking functions (Pressure Cook, Sauté, Yogurt, and Slow Cook) plus presets for some specific foods (rice, beans, meat, grains, etc.). The recipes in this book do not use the preset options. Depending on the model of Instant Pot, you'll select the cooking function by pressing a button or using a dial or touch screen.

The function used most frequently in this book is Pressure Cook (Manual on some models). After selecting Pressure Cook, you'll adjust the pressure (High or Low in all models except the LUX) and set the time.

To simmer sauces, you'll select the Sauté function, then adjust the heat level to Low, Medium, or High (Less, Normal, and More on some models). After you're finished sautéing, you'll select Cancel to stop cooking.

A STEP-BY-STEP GUIDE TO USING YOUR INSTANT POT

Most desserts are cooked "pot-in-pot"; that is, cooked in a baking dish or ramekins that are placed on the trivet inside the inner pot. For these recipes, the steps are simple:

1. Mix the ingredients and pour them into a baking dish. Often, you'll cover the dish with aluminum foil.

2. Pour water (usually 1 cup) into the pot and insert the trivet. Place the baking dish on the trivet. If the recipe requires multiple ramekins or custard cups, you may have to stack them so they all fit. Make sure they're balanced and won't tip over.

3. Lock the lid into place, making sure the lever is in the "sealing" position. Adjust the pressure and time, and start the Instant Pot. (Some models have a Start button; some begin cooking automatically.)

4. Release the pressure when cooking is completed. Some recipes will call for a "quick" (manual) pressure release, and some will allow the pressure to release naturally. A quick release depressurizes the pot all at once; you'll see a stream of vapor escaping, and it is finished when the pin drops. With natural release, the pressure drops as the temperature drops, so the dish will continue cooking during that time—it usually takes 10 to 20 minutes for the pressure to completely release. Often, you'll let the pressure release naturally for a set amount of time and then quick-release any remaining pressure.

5. After cooking, remove the baking dish. I generally use fingertip mitts to protect my hands and lift out the trivet and dish using the handles of the trivet. Unplug the Instant Pot, let the inner pot cool, empty out the water, and let it dry. Because the dessert was cooked in a covered dish, you won't even have to clean the pot or lid.

Some recipes, such as Apple-Pear Crumble (page 53), Nutty Breakfast Rice Pudding (page 27), and Tapioca Pudding (page 80), call for pressure cooking right in the inner pot. For these, there's no need to use the trivet.

Simply add the ingredients to the inner pot itself, lock the lid into place, and follow the remaining directions as given. After cooking directly in the inner pot, you'll need to empty the pot and wash it by hand or in the dishwasher. The lid is best washed by hand, with the sealing ring removed to wash it separately.

When sautéing or simmering is required either before or after pressure cooking, select the Sauté function, adjust the heat level, and cook as long as necessary. Press Cancel to end cooking, and proceed with any additional steps.

Adjusting Recipes for High-Altitude Cooking

If you remember your science lessons, you know that the higher the altitude, the lower the atmospheric pressure. For the cook, this means that the higher the altitude, the lower the boiling point of water, so the faster it will evaporate. While the sealed interior of the Instant Pot helps make up for the lower atmospheric pressure, you'll still want to adjust cooking times if you live in the mountains. For very short cooking times, there will be virtually no difference, but for longer times, some fine-tuning is necessary. The Ultra and MAX models can be set to adjust automatically for high altitudes, but if you have a different model, you'll need to increase cooking times by 5 percent for every 1,000 feet above 2,000 feet. For instance, Orange Pound Cake (page 46), which cooks for 30 minutes at sea level, would cook for 31½ minutes at 3,000 feet or 33 minutes at 4,000 feet.

EQUIPMENT ESSENTIALS

While there are a few pieces of equipment you'll need to make the recipes in this book, none of them are expensive or hard to find, and you may even have them in your kitchen already. There are both officially licensed and off-brand options available. As with all baking recipes, pan size can affect the cooking time. One note: Some metal pans will expand upon heating, so it's crucial that there's enough space (at least ¼ inch) around them, or they may get stuck in the inner pot. (Don't ask me how I know this.)

SPRINGFORM PAN: This metal or glass pan is used for dishes like cheesecake and is designed for easy dessert removal. For a 6-quart Instant Pot, you'll want a pan that's 6 to 7 inches in diameter.

7-INCH ROUND CAKE PAN: With or without a removable bottom, a cake pan is good for, well, cakes, but it can also be used for bread puddings. Choose a pan without handles, which just take up room.

SOUFFLÉ DISH (OR SIMILAR BAKING DISH): Generally made of ceramic or tempered glass, these can be used for cakes and bread pudding. For a 6-quart Instant Pot, a 1- to 1½-quart size (6½ to 7½ inches in diameter) is a good choice.

RAMEKINS OR CUSTARD CUPS: Used for individual cupcakes, muffins, puddings, or custards, ramekins can be glass or ceramic and should hold 1 to 1½ cups.

BUNDT CAKE PAN: A decorative molded cake pan is not absolutely necessary but does make for a very beautiful cake. You'll want a pan about 7 inches in diameter, holding 4 cups.

TRIVET WITH HANDLES: Newer models of the Instant Pot come with a trivet that has handles that enable you to easily remove the trivet and baking dishes. If you have an older model, your trivet may not have handles; you can buy one with handles from Instant Brands (maker of the Instant Pot) and other companies.

To prepare batters and doughs, you'll want an **ELECTRIC HAND MIXER**, a **STURDY WHISK**, and a **FLEXIBLE SPATULA**. A **FINE-MESH SIEVE** will come in handy for straining curd or custards. **FINGERTIP MITTS** and **TONGS** can be great for handling hot dishes.

STOCKING THE KITCHEN

It's easy to stock your kitchen with a collection of ingredients so you'll be able to make a delicious dessert on the fly. Many of these are shelf-stable, and some will keep for weeks in the refrigerator or months in the freezer.

REFRIGERATOR

Most of these items will last for several weeks unopened and for a week or longer after opening.

- Butter (I prefer unsalted, but salted will work, too)

- Cream cheese

- Eggs

- Fruit (lemons, limes, oranges, apples)

- Heavy cream

- Ricotta cheese

- Sour cream

- Whole milk

- Yogurt

FREEZER

Items like frozen fruits are great in desserts and will keep for months in airtight bags.

- Berries (mixed or single)

- Cherries

- Leftover bread (for bread pudding)

- Nuts (best kept in the freezer to avoid rancidity)

- Peaches

SHELF STAPLES

These baking necessities will keep indefinitely in the cupboard.

- Baking powder

- Baking soda

- Chocolate (bittersweet or semi-sweet; I like Ghirardelli chips)

- Cocoa powder

- Coconut milk

- Cornstarch

- Fine salt (fine salt, like table salt, works better in baked goods)

- Flour (all-purpose; if you use whole-wheat flour, store it in the freezer)

CONTINUED

- Rice
- Sugar (brown, white, and confectioners')
- Tapioca

SPICES

Spice mixtures, such as pumpkin pie spice, can come in handy, but I find that individual spices are more versatile. In most cases, buy them ground and keep them in a dark, cool place.

- Allspice
- Cardamom
- Cinnamon (ground and whole sticks)
- Ginger
- Nutmeg (whole is preferable)

TROUBLESHOOTING

Although the Instant Pot is a very reliable appliance, you may occasionally run across a problem in your dessert making. The following setbacks are rarely serious and almost always easily correctable.

THE POT DOESN'T COME TO PRESSURE or is leaking steam around the lid. This usually occurs if the sealing ring is not correctly seated in the lid. Make sure it fits into the groove in the lid and moves easily. Also, make sure that the lid is completely locked into place and that the steam release valve is in the "sealing" position.

I GOT A "BURN" WARNING. Instant Pots are configured with a heat sensor in the bottom of the unit. When the pot overheats, the display shows "Burn," and the pot shuts down. It's almost always triggered when there's a loss of moisture and steam doesn't build. To avoid it, make sure the lid is sealed correctly so liquid doesn't evaporate and that there is no food stuck to the bottom of the pot. If you get a "Burn" notice, scrape up any stuck food, make sure there is enough liquid, and, most important, let the pot cool down before starting to cook again.

MY DESSERT IS NOT DONE. Although cooking times in the Instant Pot are more precise than in the oven or on the stove, factors such as the temperature of ingredients can affect the cooking time. If, after the specified cook time, your dessert is *almost* done, simply replace the lid; the residual heat and steam will finish the cooking process. If your dessert is substantially underdone, lock the lid back into place and cook for another 2 to 3 minutes. For recipes such as Cinnamon-Vanilla Applesauce (page 87), select Sauté and simmer, uncovered, until done. If you plan to cook the recipe again, remember to make a note for the next time.

THERE'S LIQUID ON TOP OF MY CHEESECAKE. Because the Instant Pot cooks with pressurized steam, liquid can collect on the top of desserts, especially if they are not covered. Gently blot off the excess liquid with a paper towel or clean cheesecloth.

MY SEALING RING SMELLS LIKE GARLIC. If you also use your Instant Pot for savory cooking, you may notice some transfer of odors in the ring. Letting the ring air-dry after washing and flipping the lid up during storage so the ring stays exposed will keep that to a minimum. If you prefer, you can buy a second ring to use just for desserts.

Five Sweet Treats to Get Started

All the recipes in this book, whether they're my own creations or provided by other experienced cookbook authors, are sure to please dessert lovers of all tastes and cooking skills. Here's just a sweet sampling:

MINI CHOCOLATE MARBLE CHEESECAKES (page 30): Elegant enough for company but easy enough for a weeknight, these creamy chocolate and vanilla cheesecakes are a dream come true.

FROZEN "CREAMSICLE" MOUSSE (page 66): Orange curd is a breeze to make in the Instant Pot. Combining it with whipped cream and freezing turns it into a treat that puts ice cream to shame.

DULCE DE LECHE (page 73): Just two ingredients are all it takes to make this luscious caramel dessert, which can also be used as a delectable sauce for pound cake or cheesecake.

PEACH AND BLUEBERRY COBBLER (page 54): Fluffy, slightly sweet dumplings top an intense, jammy fruit filling in this homestyle dessert.

ESPRESSO POTS DE CRÈME (page 71): This irresistible dessert uses just six ingredients and can be prepped and cooked in under 45 minutes. It's perfect for a dinner party or a festive holiday lunch.

ABOUT THE RECIPES

The recipes begin with breakfast treats (because who doesn't like dessert for breakfast?). The remaining recipes are arranged by type of dessert (cakes, pies and fruit desserts, and custards and puddings) and end with a chapter on sauces and staples.

Although some of the prep will require a hand mixer or food processor, all the cooking is done in any Instant Pot with a capacity of 5 or more quarts. The recipes were chosen to be easy to make without many hard-to-find ingredients or expensive equipment.

To help with menu planning, these recipes include dietary labels—Dairy-Free and Nut-Free—as well as convenience labels indicating whether they can be made in 30 minutes or less (Quick) or with five or fewer ingredients, not including water, salt, or oil (5-Ingredient). To help with time management, each recipe contains an "at a glance" section summarizing how long it will take to prep, cool, cook, and release pressure; total time will include all of the steps.

My goal is to provide a wide variety of fun and easy desserts to appeal to everyone's tastes and cooking experience. I truly hope you enjoy them!

CHAPTER 2

BREAKFAST DESSERTS

BROWNED-BUTTER APPLE SPICE CAKE

SERVES 6 | PREP PLUS COOLING TIME: 30 MINUTES | SAUTÉ: 5 MINUTES

PRESSURE COOK: 18 MINUTES, HIGH | RELEASE: NATURAL FOR 10 MINUTES, THEN QUICK

TOTAL TIME: 1 HOUR 20 MINUTES

The combination of browned butter, cinnamon, and cardamom is delicious in all kinds of desserts, especially this one. This recipe produces a very moist cake and makes a wonderful dessert, but because it contains fruit and yogurt, you can sneak it in for breakfast.

4 tablespoons unsalted butter, plus
  more for greasing

1 large egg

1 cup European or Greek Yogurt
  (page 90) or store-bought plain
  Greek yogurt

⅓ cup granulated sugar

1 teaspoon pure vanilla extract

1 cup all-purpose flour

1½ teaspoons baking powder

¼ teaspoon ground cinnamon

⅛ teaspoon ground cardamom

1 medium apple, peeled, cored, and diced

1 cup water, for steaming

¼ cup confectioners' sugar

1. Lightly grease a 6- or 7-inch springform pan with butter and set aside.
2. Select Sauté and adjust the heat to Medium. Put the remaining 4 tablespoons of butter in the inner pot and cook until the milk solids begin to brown, 3 to 5 minutes (see Tip). Select Cancel.
3. Pour the browned butter into a large bowl. Stir in the egg, yogurt, sugar, and vanilla. In a small bowl, sift together the flour, baking powder, cinnamon, and cardamom. Add the dry ingredients to the wet ingredients, and stir until just combined. Stir in the apple. Pour the batter into the prepared pan. Cover with aluminum foil.
4. Wipe the butter out of the inner pot and return it to the base. Pour the water into the inner pot and insert the trivet. Place the pan on the trivet. Secure the lid.

5. Select Pressure Cook or Manual, adjust the pressure to High, and set the time to 18 minutes. When cooking is complete, naturally release the pressure for 10 minutes, then quick-release remaining pressure. Unlock and remove the lid.
6. Remove the pan, then remove the foil. Let the cake cool for 5 to 10 minutes, then release the sides of the pan. Let the cake cool for another 10 minutes. Dust with the confectioners' sugar and serve.

TIP: Browning the butter adds a complex nutty flavor to this cake, but it's also delicious with melted butter (not browned) if you want to save a little time.

RAMEKIN CINNAMON COFFEE CAKES

SERVES 5 | PREP TIME: 10 MINUTES | PRESSURE COOK: 6 MINUTES, HIGH | RELEASE: QUICK
TOTAL TIME: 25 MINUTES

No need to stop on the way to work to inhale sometimes-stale coffee cake from your coffee shop counter. These perfectly spiced treats come together in minutes, make a perfect grab-and-go breakfast, and taste as heavenly as if they came from your favorite bakery.

FOR THE BATTER

1 cup all-purpose flour
⅓ cup granulated sugar
1 teaspoon ground cinnamon
½ teaspoon fine salt
½ teaspoon baking powder
½ teaspoon baking soda
1 cup European or Greek Yogurt
   (page 90) or store-bought plain
   Greek yogurt

4 tablespoons butter, melted
1 large egg
1 teaspoon pure vanilla extract
Nonstick cooking spray

FOR THE TOPPING

2 tablespoons packed light brown sugar
2 tablespoons chopped walnuts
1 tablespoon butter

½ teaspoon ground cinnamon
1 cup water

1. **MAKE THE BATTER:** In a large bowl, mix the flour, granulated sugar, cinnamon, salt, baking powder, and baking soda until well blended. Add the yogurt, melted butter, egg, and vanilla, and stir to combine. Lightly spray 5 (4-inch) ramekins with cooking spray, and divide the batter among the ramekins, filling each one almost to the top.

2. **MAKE THE TOPPING:** In a small bowl, stir together the brown sugar, walnuts, butter, and cinnamon. Place a spoonful of topping in each ramekin, and cover each with aluminum foil.

3. **MAKE THE COFFEE CAKES:** Pour the water into the inner pot and insert the trivet. Arrange the ramekins on the trivet, stacking as necessary. Secure the lid.

4. Select Pressure Cook or Manual, adjust the pressure to High, and set the time to 6 minutes. When cooking is complete, quick-release the pressure. Unlock and remove the lid.

5. Use an oven mitt or tongs to remove the ramekins, uncover, and serve.

TIP: Refrigerate in a sealed container for up to 5 days.

CHOCOLATE CHIP BANANA BREAD

SERVES 2 | PREP PLUS COOLING TIME: 55 MINUTES | PRESSURE COOK: 40 MINUTES, HIGH
RELEASE: NATURAL FOR 18 MINUTES | TOTAL TIME: 2 HOURS

Unlike banana bread that is cooked in the oven, this version is considerably denser (more filling) than a traditional loaf of quick bread, but it's just as delicious. Steaming versus baking really brings out the fresh banana flavor, and cutting down the fat with applesauce makes each bite feel a little less guilt-ridden.

1 cup water
3 tablespoons unsalted butter, at room
   temperature, plus more for greasing
¼ cup applesauce
2 tablespoons packed brown sugar
1 egg, at room temperature
2 very ripe bananas, mashed

¼ cup whole milk
½ teaspoon pure vanilla extract
1 cup all-purpose flour
1 teaspoon baking soda
¼ teaspoon kosher salt
⅓ cup chocolate chips

1. Pour the water into the inner pot and insert the trivet. Grease a 7-inch loaf pan with butter and set aside.
2. In a medium bowl, mix together 3 tablespoons of butter, the applesauce, and the brown sugar. Whisk in the egg; then stir in the bananas, milk, and vanilla. Stir in the flour, baking soda, and salt. Fold in the chocolate chips. Pour the batter into the prepared loaf pan, cover with aluminum foil, and place on the trivet inside the pot. Secure the lid.
3. Select Pressure Cook or Manual, adjust the pressure to High, and set the time to 40 minutes. When cooking is complete, allow the pressure to naturally release. Unlock and remove the lid.
4. Carefully remove the pan and place it on a cooling rack. Remove the foil, being sure to avoid dripping any condensation onto the bread. Test the bread with a toothpick; no more than a few moist crumbs should cling to it. If it's not cooked through, place the bread back in the Instant Pot, cover with the foil again, and set on High pressure for another 5 minutes, ending with a quick release. Let it cool at room temperature for 45 minutes. Once cool, cut into thick slices and enjoy.

CHALLAH BREAD PUDDING

SERVES 4 TO 6 | PREP TIME: 10 MINUTES | PRESSURE COOK: 20 MINUTES, LOW
RELEASE: NATURAL FOR 10 MINUTES, THEN QUICK | TOTAL TIME: 50 MINUTES

The Instant Pot will change the way you feel about making brunch for a large group because it makes it so easy to whip up a big pot of sweet deliciousness with very little effort. This dish is comfort food at its best.

1 cup water
1 tablespoon butter, for greasing
8 slices challah bread, cut into 1-inch cubes
3 large eggs
1 cup whole milk

⅓ cup pure maple syrup
2 teaspoons pure vanilla extract
1 tablespoon ground cinnamon (optional)
½ teaspoon ground nutmeg (optional)
Pinch fine salt

1. Pour the water into the inner pot and insert the trivet. Use the butter to grease a 7-inch baking dish. Fill the dish with the bread cubes.
2. In a small bowl, whisk the eggs, milk, syrup, vanilla, cinnamon (if using), nutmeg (if using), and salt until just combined.
3. Pour the egg mixture over the bread, and let it sit until the bread is fully soaked, about 5 minutes. Cover with aluminum foil, and lower the baking dish onto the trivet. Secure the lid.
4. Select Pressure Cook or Manual, adjust the pressure to Low, and set the time to 20 minutes. When cooking is complete, allow the pressure to naturally release for 10 minutes, then quick-release any remaining pressure. Unlock and remove the lid.
5. Remove the baking dish, then remove the foil. Serve warm.

TIP: Fresh challah is the best choice for this recipe, but you can use any light-textured bread you have on hand. Avoid anything dense or with a tough crust.

CLAFOUTIS

SERVES 2 | PREP PLUS COOLING TIME: 15 MINUTES | PRESSURE COOK: 11 MINUTES, HIGH
RELEASE: QUICK | TOTAL TIME: 35 MINUTES

Clafoutis is a classic French dessert, but I've always loved it for breakfast. It combines all of the best parts of custard, soufflé, and cake. You can also use frozen fruit, making it an option all year long.

1 teaspoon butter, for greasing
½ cup fresh or frozen pitted cherries
⅓ cup whole milk
3 tablespoons heavy cream
3 tablespoons granulated sugar
¼ cup all-purpose flour
1 large egg

¼ teaspoon pure vanilla extract
¼ teaspoon grated lemon zest
Pinch fine salt
1 cup water
2 teaspoons confectioners' sugar,
   for serving

1. Grease 2 (1-cup) ramekins or custard cups with the butter. Divide the cherries between the ramekins.
2. In a medium mixing bowl, combine the milk, cream, sugar, flour, egg, vanilla, lemon zest, and salt. Using a hand mixer, beat the ingredients on medium speed until the batter is smooth, about 2 minutes. Pour the batter over the berries; the ramekins should be filled about three-quarters of the way with batter.
3. Pour the water into the inner pot and insert the trivet. Place the ramekins on the trivet and lay a piece of aluminum foil over them (but don't crimp it down; it's just to keep steam from condensing on the surface). Secure the lid.
4. Select Pressure Cook or Manual, adjust the pressure to High, and set the time to 11 minutes. When cooking is complete, quick-release the pressure. Unlock and remove the lid.
5. Using tongs, remove the foil, then remove the ramekins from the Instant Pot. Let the clafoutis cool for at least 5 minutes. Sift confectioners' sugar over the surface of each clafoutis. Serve warm.

TIP: While clafoutis is traditionally made with cherries, it's also delicious with any fresh or frozen berries.

BLUEBERRY-OATMEAL MUFFINS

SERVES 4 | PREP PLUS COOLING TIME: 30 MINUTES | PRESSURE COOK: 12 MINUTES, HIGH
RELEASE: NATURAL FOR 10 MINUTES, THEN QUICK | TOTAL TIME: 1 HOUR

These moist, blueberry-studded muffins are a wonderful way to start the morning. The hearty oats, along with their blueberry counterparts, add some much-needed antioxidants to what tastes like a treat.

1 egg
¼ cup European or Greek Yogurt (page 90) or store-bought plain Greek yogurt
¼ cup packed brown sugar
3 tablespoons butter, melted
½ teaspoon pure vanilla extract
⅓ cup quick oats

½ cup all-purpose flour
½ teaspoon baking powder
¼ teaspoon baking soda
Pinch kosher salt
½ cup fresh blueberries
Nonstick cooking spray
1 cup water

1. In a medium bowl, stir together the egg, yogurt, brown sugar, butter, and vanilla. In a separate bowl, whisk together the oats, flour, baking powder, baking soda, and salt, and add to the wet ingredients. Stir just until combined. Gently fold in the blueberries.
2. Generously spray 4 ramekins or custard cups with cooking spray. Pour the batter evenly into the prepared ramekins. Loosely cover each ramekin with foil.
3. Pour the water into the inner pot and insert the trivet. Arrange the ramekins on the trivet, stacking if necessary. Secure the lid.
4. Select Pressure Cook or Manual, adjust the pressure to High, and set the time to 12 minutes. When cooking is complete, let the pressure release naturally for 10 minutes, then quick-release any remaining pressure. Unlock and remove the lid.
5. Use tongs to carefully remove the ramekins. Remove the foil. Let the muffins cool for 10 minutes, then run a knife around the inside of each ramekin. Invert the ramekins to release the muffins, and serve.

TIP: Make a double batch of these treats on the weekend and freeze them for up to 1 month. Let them thaw 2 to 3 hours or overnight before serving.

NUT-FREE

SPICED PEACH FRENCH TOAST CUPS

SERVES 4 | PREP TIME: 10 MINUTES | PRESSURE COOK: 8 MINUTES, HIGH
RELEASE: NATURAL FOR 5 MINUTES, THEN QUICK | TOTAL TIME: 30 MINUTES

Filled with peaches and warm spices, these delicious little bites are a cross between French toast and bread pudding. They boast the best parts of each. You can even make these ahead of time and rewarm them in the Instant Pot or a skillet (see Tip).

1 tablespoon butter, for greasing
2 large eggs
1 cup whole milk
¼ cup heavy cream
¼ teaspoon pure vanilla extract
Pinch fine salt
½ teaspoon ground cinnamon

½ teaspoon ground cardamom
4 cups (¾-inch cubes) sandwich bread
   (4 to 5 slices)
1 ripe peach, peeled and chopped
1 cup water
Confectioners' sugar or pure maple
   syrup, for serving

1. Grease 4 small ramekins or custard cups with the butter.
2. In a medium bowl, whisk the eggs until the yolks and whites are completely mixed. Add the milk, cream, vanilla, salt, cinnamon, and cardamom, and whisk to combine. Add the bread cubes and gently stir to coat with the egg mixture. Let sit for 2 to 3 minutes to let the bread absorb some of the custard.
3. Add the chopped peach to the bowl and gently stir again. Spoon the mixture evenly into the ramekins. Cover each with aluminum foil.
4. Pour 1 cup of water into the inner pot and insert the trivet. Arrange the ramekins on top, stacking if necessary. Secure the lid.
5. Select Pressure Cook or Manual, adjust the pressure to High, and set the time to 8 minutes. When cooking is complete, let the pressure release naturally for 5 minutes, then quick-release the remaining pressure. Unlock and remove the lid.

6. Use tongs to remove the ramekins. Remove the foil. Let the French toast cool for a few minutes before serving topped with confectioners' sugar or syrup.

TIP: To make these more like traditional French toast, after removing the ramekins from the Instant Pot, melt 2 tablespoons butter in a large skillet or griddle. Unmold the cooked French toasts. When the butter has just stopped foaming, place the French toasts in the skillet, cook over medium heat until golden brown, about 2 minutes per side, and serve.

NUTTY BREAKFAST RICE PUDDING

SERVES 6 | PREP TIME: 10 MINUTES | PRESSURE COOK: 5 MINUTES, HIGH | RELEASE: NATURAL FOR 10 MINUTES, THEN QUICK | SAUTÉ TIME: 5 MINUTES | TOTAL TIME: 40 MINUTES

Rice pudding, popular all over the world, has disputed origins, having been created in either China or India centuries ago. This modern, Instant Pot version is a little less sweet than most but rich and satisfying; the nuts add a little protein as well as a delightful crunch.

¾ cup arborio rice
1 cup water
¼ teaspoon fine salt
1 cinnamon stick
1¼ cups whole milk, divided
2 tablespoons heavy cream

¼ cup granulated sugar, or
 more to taste
1 large egg
½ teaspoon pure vanilla extract
¾ cup chopped roasted unsalted
 pistachios

1. Put the rice in the inner pot, then add the water, salt, cinnamon, and ¼ cup of milk. Stir to combine. Secure the lid.
2. Select Pressure Cook or Manual, adjust the pressure to High, and set the time to 5 minutes. When cooking is complete, let the pressure release naturally for 10 minutes, then quick-release any remaining pressure. Unlock and remove the lid. Remove the cinnamon stick.
3. In a small bowl, whisk together the remaining 1 cup of milk and the cream, sugar, egg, and vanilla until the mixture is smooth.
4. Select Sauté and adjust the heat to Medium. Stir the milk mixture into the cooked rice and bring to a simmer, stirring constantly. Cook for 1 to 2 minutes, until the rice pudding is thickened and smooth. Taste and adjust the sweetness, letting the pudding cook until any additional sugar dissolves. Select Cancel.
5. Let it cool slightly, then serve topped with the pistachios.

TIP: Rice pudding will thicken as it cools, so if you prefer a thicker pudding, let it come to room temperature before serving.

CHAPTER 3

CAKES

MINI CHOCOLATE MARBLE CHEESECAKES

**SERVES 4 | PREP PLUS COOLING TIME: 35 MINUTES | PRESSURE COOK: 6 MINUTES, HIGH
RELEASE: NATURAL FOR 8 MINUTES THEN QUICK | TOTAL TIME: 55 MINUTES, PLUS 3 HOURS TO CHILL**

There's nothing quite like chocolate cheesecake to end a romantic meal. Oh, let's be honest: There's nothing quite like chocolate cheesecake, period. And making these mini versions in the Instant Pot is seamless and easy. The swirl of vanilla batter on top of chocolate reverses the usual marble effect and is particularly beautiful.

FOR THE CRUST

½ cup chocolate wafer cookie crumbs (from about 12 cookies)

2 tablespoons unsalted butter, melted

FOR THE FILLING

6 ounces cream cheese, at room temperature

1 tablespoon sour cream

½ teaspoon pure vanilla extract

¼ cup granulated sugar

1 large egg

3 ounces dark chocolate chips, melted

1 cup water

1. **MAKE THE CRUST:** In a medium bowl, mix the cookie crumbs with the butter. Scoop out about 2 tablespoons of the crumb mixture into each of 4 (1-cup) ramekins or custard cups, and press it down to make a layer ¼ inch thick. (You may not need all the crumbs; you can reserve the rest and sprinkle over the top of the cheesecakes as garnish.)

2. **MAKE THE FILLING:** In a small bowl, beat the cream cheese, sour cream, and vanilla with a hand mixer until smooth. Add the sugar gradually, continuing to beat until the mixture is smooth again.

3. Beat in the egg until fully incorporated. Reserve 2 tablespoons of the batter in another small bowl, then mix the melted chocolate into the larger amount of batter.

4. Divide the chocolate cheesecake batter among the ramekins. Spoon the reserved vanilla batter over the chocolate mixture, and swirl a skewer or small knife through it to create a marbled pattern.

5. **MAKE THE CHEESECAKES:** Pour 1 cup of water into the inner pot and insert the trivet. Arrange the ramekins on the trivet, stacking them if necessary. Lay a piece of aluminum foil over the ramekins to keep condensation off the top of the cheesecakes. Secure the lid.

6. Select Pressure Cook or Manual, adjust the pressure to High, and set the time to 6 minutes. When cooking is complete, let the pressure release naturally for 8 minutes, then quick-release any remaining pressure. Unlock and remove the lid.

7. Use tongs to remove the foil, then remove the ramekins from the Instant Pot. Let the cheesecakes cool for 20 minutes, then refrigerate to chill thoroughly, 3 to 4 hours.

TIP: I like to use Guittard brand 60 percent chocolate chips, but any dark chocolate chips will work.

FRUITY CHEESECAKE WITH CHOCOLATE COOKIE CRUST

SERVES 6 TO 8 | PREP PLUS COOLING TIME: 30 MINUTES | PRESSURE COOK: 25 MINUTES, HIGH
RELEASE: NATURAL FOR 10 MINUTES, THEN QUICK | TOTAL TIME: 1 HOUR 25 MINUTES,
PLUS 3 HOURS TO CHILL

If you've never made cheesecake in the Instant Pot, this gorgeous and tasty dessert recipe will convert you. Try this recipe with strawberry, blackberry, and blueberry fruit spread, too—all are delicious!

10 chocolate sandwich cookies, filling removed and reserved
Nonstick cooking spray
1 (8-ounce) package cream cheese
1 large egg

2 tablespoons raspberry or pomegranate jam
1 cup water
Fresh raspberries or pomegranate seeds, for garnish

1. Put the cookies in the bowl of a food processor and blend to a sand-like consistency.
2. Spray a 6-inch springform pan with cooking spray, and press the cookie crumbs into the bottom of the pan to form a crust.
3. In a medium bowl, combine the reserved cookie filling, cream cheese, and egg. Mix until well combined.
4. Pour the mixture into the prepared pan and spread evenly. Add the fruit jam in dollops and, using a knife or chopstick, swirl to make a design. Cover with aluminum foil.
5. Pour the water into the inner pot and insert the trivet. Carefully place the pan on the trivet. Secure the lid.
6. Select Pressure Cook or Manual, adjust the pressure to High, and set the time to 25 minutes. When cooking is complete, let the pressure release naturally for 10 minutes, then quick-release any remaining pressure. Unlock and remove the lid.
7. Carefully remove the pan, then remove the foil. Let the cheesecake sit at room temperature for about 20 minutes, then transfer to the refrigerator to chill completely, 3 to 4 hours. Garnish with raspberries or pomegranate seeds before serving.

CHOCOLATE COOKIE CHEESECAKE

SERVES 6 TO 10 | PREP TIME: 10 MINUTES | PRESSURE COOK: 35 MINUTES, HIGH

RELEASE: NATURAL FOR 18 MINUTES | TOTAL TIME: 1 HOUR 5 MINUTES, PLUS 6 HOURS TO CHILL

This version of cheesecake is smooth, silky, rich, chocolaty, and ready to impress. It is the perfect dessert to make for company of all ages, ideal to bring for any gathering, and a lovely gift for chocolate-loving friends.

FOR THE CRUST

Nonstick cooking spray

½ cup chocolate sandwich cookie crumbs (from 8 to 10 cookies)

3 tablespoons butter, melted

FOR THE FILLING

2 (8-ounce) packages full-fat cream cheese, at room temperature

½ cup sour cream, at room temperature

¾ cup granulated sugar

2 tablespoons unsweetened cocoa powder

½ teaspoon sea salt

2 tablespoons pure vanilla extract

1 tablespoon cornstarch

3 large eggs

FOR MAKING AND SERVING THE CHEESECAKE

1 cup water

½ cup chocolate sandwich cookie crumbs, for topping

1. **MAKE THE CRUST:** Coat the bottom of a 7-inch springform pan with cooking spray. In a medium bowl, mix the cookie crumbs and melted butter together, and press the mixture evenly into the bottom of the prepared pan.
2. **MAKE THE FILLING:** In a medium bowl, beat the cream cheese, sour cream, sugar, cocoa, salt, vanilla, and cornstarch until well blended. Beat in the eggs just until incorporated. Do not overmix. Spoon the cream cheese mixture over the crust, and cover the pan with aluminum foil.
3. **MAKE AND SERVE THE CHEESECAKE:** Pour the water into the inner pot and insert the trivet. Carefully place the pan on the trivet. Secure the lid.
4. Select Pressure Cook or Manual, adjust the pressure to High, and set the time to 35 minutes. When cooking is complete, allow the pressure to naturally release. Unlock and remove the lid.
5. Carefully lift out the pan using the handles of the trivet. Refrigerate the cheesecake, covered, for 6 to 8 hours to chill and set up.
6. Remove the foil and release the sides of the pan. Top with the cookie crumbs, cut into slices, and serve.

TIP: Refrigerate in a sealed container for up to 3 days.

STEEL-CUT OAT CAKE

SERVES 4 TO 6 | PREP PLUS COOLING TIME: 15 MINUTES | PRESSURE COOK: 25 MINUTES, HIGH RELEASE: NATURAL FOR 10 MINUTES, THEN QUICK | TOTAL TIME: 1 HOUR

This cake is almost like a chewy granola bar. It makes a not-too-sweet dessert or a healthy snack. The recipe-changing ingredient, chai concentrate, is just what it sounds like: the spices used in chai (cinnamon, cloves, cardamom, etc.) steeped in hot water. It's available in supermarkets and online, but if you can't find it, simply substitute vanilla extract and a dash of pumpkin pie spice.

1½ teaspoons butter, for greasing
1 cup water
2 cups whole milk
¼ cup honey
Pinch fine salt

2 teaspoons chai concentrate (or ½ teaspoon pure vanilla extract and a dash of pumpkin pie spice)
1 cup steel-cut oats
¼ cup raisins or diced dried fruit medley

1. Grease a 7-inch baking dish with the butter and set aside.
2. Pour the water into the inner pot and insert the trivet.
3. In a mixing bowl, whisk together the milk, honey, salt, and chai concentrate until very well combined. Add the oats and raisins, and whisk until just combined.
4. Pour the oat mixture into the prepared baking dish. Cover with aluminum foil and place on the trivet. Secure the lid.
5. Select Pressure Cook or Manual, adjust the pressure to High, and set the time to 25 minutes. When cooking is complete, allow the pressure to release naturally for 10 minutes, then quick-release any remaining pressure. Unlock and remove the lid.
6. Remove the baking dish and let it sit for 5 minutes before removing the foil. Invert the cake onto a plate and cut into wedges to serve.

TIP: If you want to make this recipe dairy-free, coat the baking dish with oil and use 1¾ cups almond milk in place of the 2 cups whole milk.

GINGERBREAD CUPCAKES

SERVES 4 | PREP PLUS COOLING TIME: 35 MINUTES | PRESSURE COOK: 10 MINUTES, HIGH RELEASE: QUICK | TOTAL TIME: 1 HOUR

These tasty cupcakes are moist and spicy, just like old-fashioned gingerbread. I love them topped with whipped cream, but they're also good with the glaze from Orange Pound Cake (page 46) or the frosting from Carrot-Zucchini Cake (page 48).

3 tablespoons very hot water
¼ cup vegetable oil
¼ cup packed light brown sugar
¼ cup molasses
1 egg
⅔ cup all-purpose flour
¼ teaspoon fine salt

¼ teaspoon baking powder
¼ teaspoon baking soda
¾ teaspoon ground ginger
½ teaspoon ground cinnamon
Nonstick cooking spray
1 cup water
Sweetened whipped cream, for topping

1. In a small bowl, use a hand mixer to combine the hot water, oil, brown sugar, molasses, and egg.
2. In a separate bowl, whisk together the flour, salt, baking powder, baking soda, ginger, and cinnamon, and add them to the liquid mixture. Mix on medium speed until the ingredients are thoroughly combined, with no lumps.
3. Spray 4 (1-cup) ramekins or custard cups with cooking spray. Pour the batter into the prepared ramekins.
4. Pour the water into the inner pot and insert the trivet. Arrange the ramekins on the trivet, stacking as necessary, and lay a piece of aluminum foil over the ramekins (don't crimp it down; it's just to keep steam from condensing on the surface). Secure the lid.
5. Select Pressure Cook or Manual, adjust the pressure to High, and set the time to 10 minutes. When cooking is complete, quick-release the pressure. Unlock and remove the lid.
6. Using tongs, remove the foil, then remove the ramekins. Let the cupcakes cool for at least 10 minutes, flip them out of the ramekins, and serve topped with whipped cream.

CARAMELIZED BANANA UPSIDE-DOWN CAKE

SERVES 8 | PREP PLUS COOLING TIME: 45 MINUTES | PRESSURE COOK: 30 MINUTES, HIGH
RELEASE: NATURAL FOR 5 MINUTES, THEN QUICK | TOTAL TIME: 1 HOUR 30 MINUTES

Sure, pineapple upside-down cake gets all the glory, but it's time to update this classic. Caramelized bananas make the most delectable addition to this moist, luscious cake with its hints of cinnamon and cardamom.

½ cup plus 3 tablespoons unsalted butter, at room temperature, divided
¼ cup plus 2 tablespoons packed dark brown sugar, divided
2 medium bananas, sliced ¼ inch thick
1 cup granulated sugar
2 large eggs
1 teaspoon pure vanilla extract

1½ cups all-purpose flour
2 teaspoons baking powder
½ teaspoon ground cinnamon
½ teaspoon ground cardamom
¼ teaspoon fine salt
¾ cup whole milk
1 cup water

1. Spread 1 tablespoon of butter on the bottom of a 7-inch cake pan, using a little to coat the sides of the pan but leaving a heavy coat on the bottom. Sprinkle 2 tablespoons of brown sugar over the bottom of the pan. Arrange the banana slices in a single layer in the bottom of the pan, packing them as tightly as possible. Depending on the size of the bananas, you may not need all the slices.
2. In a small bowl, mix the remaining ¼ cup brown sugar with 2 tablespoons of butter, mashing together with a fork. Use your fingers to break the mixture into small pieces and sprinkle over the bananas. Set aside.
3. In a large bowl, combine the remaining ½ cup of butter and the granulated sugar. With a hand mixer, beat until creamy and light colored, about 2 minutes. Add the eggs and vanilla, and beat until well combined.
4. In a medium bowl, whisk together the flour, baking powder, cinnamon, cardamom, and salt.

5. Add about one-third of the flour mixture to the butter and sugar, and mix on low speed. Add half the milk, and mix again. Repeat with another one-third of the flour mixture and the remaining milk. Add the remaining flour mixture, and mix.
6. Carefully pour the batter over the bananas. Cover the pan with aluminum foil.
7. Pour the water into the inner pot and insert the trivet. Place the cake pan on the trivet. Secure the lid.
8. Select Pressure Cook or Manual, adjust the pressure to High, and set the time to 30 minutes. When cooking is complete, let the pressure release naturally for 5 minutes, then quick-release any remaining pressure. Unlock and remove the lid.
9. Carefully remove the pan, then remove the foil. Let the cake cool for 30 minutes. Run a thin-bladed spatula or knife around the inside of the pan. Place a plate over the pan and invert, shaking gently to release the cake. If any bananas stick, don't worry. Carefully remove them with a small spatula and return them to the top of the cake.

TIP: When cooked, bananas turn a sort of burgundy color, which may be surprising. As the cake sits, they'll darken even further. So while the cake is delicious, it's a bit homely looking. If you like, you can dust the top with confectioners' sugar or drizzle it with a bit of store-bought or homemade caramel.

CRANBERRY POLENTA CAKE

SERVES 6 | PREP PLUS COOLING TIME: 25 MINUTES | PRESSURE COOK: 35 MINUTES, HIGH
RELEASE: NATURAL FOR 10 MINUTES, THEN QUICK | TOTAL TIME: 1 HOUR 20 MINUTES

Polenta is a gluten-free, ground form of corn chock-full of anti-oxidants. In this recipe, it is the base of a sweet, tangy, fruit-studded version of cornbread, perfect for brunch.

½ cup dried cranberries
½ cup orange juice
1½ cups fine polenta (not instant or quick-cook) or cornmeal
½ cup all-purpose flour
1 tablespoon baking powder
½ cup granulated sugar
½ teaspoon fine salt
2 large eggs

½ cup European or Greek Yogurt (page 90) or store-bought plain Greek yogurt
½ cup whole milk
8 tablespoons (1 stick) unsalted butter, melted
Nonstick cooking spray
1 cup water
2 to 3 tablespoons confectioners' sugar, for dusting

1. Put the cranberries in a small bowl, and pour the orange juice over them. Set aside.
2. In a large bowl, combine the polenta, flour, baking powder, sugar, and salt. In a medium bowl, thoroughly whisk together the eggs, yogurt, and milk. Stir into the dry ingredients. Add the melted butter and stir to combine. Drain the cranberries and gently stir them into the batter.
3. Spray a 7-inch springform pan with cooking spray. Pour the batter into the prepared pan and spread it out evenly. Cover the pan with aluminum foil.
4. Pour the water into the inner pot and insert the trivet. Place the pan on the trivet. Secure the lid.
5. Select Pressure Cook or Manual, adjust the pressure to High, and set the time to 35 minutes. When cooking is complete, let the pressure release naturally for 10 minutes, then quick-release any remaining pressure. Unlock and remove the lid.
6. Carefully remove the pan, then remove the foil. Let the cake cool for 10 minutes, then release the sides of the pan. Dust with the confectioners' sugar.

PLUM PUDDING CAKE

SERVES 6 | PREP PLUS COOLING TIME: 30 MINUTES | PRESSURE COOK: 20 MINUTES, HIGH
RELEASE: NATURAL FOR 10 MINUTES, THEN QUICK | TOTAL TIME: 1 HOUR 15 MINUTES

Not to be confused with British plum pudding (which actually contains no plums!), this tasty dessert combines the best of cake, pudding, and soufflé.

¾ cup all-purpose flour
½ teaspoon baking soda
¼ teaspoon fine salt
1 teaspoon ground cinnamon
½ teaspoon allspice
½ cup packed light brown sugar
4 tablespoons unsalted butter, melted
3 large eggs, yolks and whites separated
¾ cup whole milk

2 tablespoons freshly squeezed lemon juice
12 ounces (3 to 4) Damson, Santa Rosa, or Moyer plums, pitted and cut into eighths
Nonstick cooking spray
1 cup water
Whipped cream or confectioners' sugar, for serving

1. In a small bowl, whisk together the flour, baking soda, salt, cinnamon, and allspice. In a large bowl, whisk together the brown sugar, butter, egg yolks, milk, and lemon juice. Stir the flour mixture into the wet ingredients, and mix until no lumps remain.
2. In a medium bowl, whip the egg whites until soft peaks form. Fold them into the batter. Gently fold in the plums.
3. Spray a 7-inch soufflé dish or cake pan with cooking spray. Pour the batter into the pan and cover with aluminum foil.
4. Pour the water into the inner pot and insert the trivet. Place the pan on the trivet. Secure the lid.
5. Select Pressure Cook or Manual, adjust the pressure to High, and set the time to 20 minutes. When cooking is complete, let the pressure release naturally for 10 minutes, then quick-release any remaining pressure. Unlock and remove the lid.
6. Remove the pan, then remove the foil. Let the cake cool for 15 to 20 minutes. Serve warm with whipped cream or confectioners' sugar.

TIP: Can't find plums? Peaches are also delicious in this recipe, but you'll want to peel them before pitting and slicing.

CHOCOLATE-HAZELNUT LAVA CAKES

SERVES 2 | PREP PLUS COOLING TIME: 15 MINUTES | PRESSURE COOK: 9 MINUTES, HIGH
RELEASE: QUICK | TOTAL TIME: 35 MINUTES

Flourless cake meets soufflé in these ultrarich and decadent individual-size lava cakes. Once flipped onto a serving plate, the little cakes might not win any beauty contests (pressure cooking can cause uneven rising), but the gooey chocolate-and-hazelnut goodness will not disappoint, proving that looks aren't everything.

1 cup water
1 tablespoon butter, for greasing
2 ounces bittersweet chocolate, chopped
1 egg
1 egg yolk
2 tablespoons granulated sugar
¼ cup hazelnut spread

3 tablespoons all-purpose flour
Pinch fine salt
Confectioners' sugar, for serving
Vanilla ice cream or whipped cream, for serving
Chopped toasted hazelnuts, for serving
Sliced strawberries, for serving

1. Pour the water into the inner pot and insert the trivet. Grease 2 (1-cup) ramekins with the butter and set aside.
2. In a microwave-safe bowl, melt the chocolate in 30-second bursts, stirring with a rubber spatula at the end of each one until smooth. (Alternatively, set the bowl over a double boiler.) Let it cool.
3. In a medium bowl, whisk the egg and egg yolk until smooth. Add the granulated sugar and whisk well. Add the hazelnut spread and cooled chocolate and mix with a rubber spatula until smooth. Gently fold in the flour and salt until no streaks remain.
4. Spoon the batter into the prepared ramekins, dividing it evenly. Set the ramekins on the trivet. Secure the lid.

CONTINUED

5. Select Pressure Cook or Manual, adjust the pressure to High, and set the time to 9 minutes. When cooking is complete, quick-release the pressure in the pot. Unlock and remove the lid.

6. Using tongs, carefully remove the ramekins from the pot and transfer them to a rack to cool for 5 minutes. When ready to serve, turn the cakes out onto individual serving plates and dust with confectioners' sugar. Serve with a scoop of high-quality vanilla ice cream or whipped cream, toasted hazelnuts, and sliced strawberries.

TIP: For a nut-free version, replace the hazelnut spread with an equal amount of butter. The results will be slightly less rich but equally tasty.

BLISSFUL BROWNIES

SERVES 6 | PREP PLUS COOLING TIME: 40 MINUTES | PRESSURE COOK: 35 MINUTES, HIGH
RELEASE: NATURAL FOR 18 MINUTES | TOTAL TIME: 1 HOUR 35 MINUTES

However you like your brownies—plain, sprinkled with salt, or topped with ice cream—this recipe will surely meet your chocolate cravings. While brownies cooked in an Instant Pot do have a different texture than conventionally baked brownies, the chocolaty goodness is just as (some might even say *more*) satisfying.

1 cup all-purpose flour
¼ cup cocoa powder
¾ cup confectioners' sugar
1 teaspoon baking powder
½ teaspoon baking soda
¼ cup European or Greek Yogurt
   (page 90) or store-bought plain
   Greek yogurt

½ cup whole milk
3 tablespoons vegetable oil,
   plus 1 teaspoon
2 cups water
2 teaspoons flaky salt, such as Maldon
   (optional)

1. In a large bowl, sift together the flour, cocoa powder, and sugar. Add the baking powder and baking soda, and mix to combine.
2. In a medium bowl, whisk together the yogurt, milk, and 3 tablespoons of oil.
3. Little by little, add the wet ingredients to the dry ingredients, gently folding them together with each addition to form a smooth batter. Grease a springform pan with the remaining 1 teaspoon of oil. Pour the batter into the pan, and tightly cover with aluminum foil.
4. Pour the water into the inner pot and insert the trivet. Place the pan on the trivet. Secure the lid.
5. Select Pressure Cook or Manual, adjust the pressure to High, and set the time to 35 minutes. When cooking is complete, naturally release the pressure. Unlock and remove the lid.
6. Remove the pan, then remove the foil. Sprinkle the brownies with the flaky salt (if using), and let them cool for at least 30 minutes. Gently remove them from the pan, slice, and serve.

ORANGE POUND CAKE

SERVES 8 | PREP PLUS COOLING TIME: 45 MINUTES | PRESSURE COOK: 30 MINUTES, HIGH
RELEASE: NATURAL FOR 15 MINUTES, THEN QUICK | TOTAL TIME: 1 HOUR 45 MINUTES

Rich and buttery, pound cake comes out beautifully in the Instant Pot. This recipe includes an irresistible orange glaze, but if you prefer to leave it unglazed, it's a perfect base for fresh fruit and whipped cream, and it's also great toasted and spread with Ginger Pear Butter (page 89).

8 tablespoons (1 stick) unsalted butter, at room temperature
¾ cup granulated sugar
1 teaspoon pure vanilla extract
1½ teaspoons finely grated orange zest
2 eggs, at room temperature
1¼ cups all-purpose flour
½ teaspoon baking powder
¼ teaspoon baking soda
⅛ teaspoon fine salt
2 tablespoons plain whole-milk yogurt
3 tablespoons orange juice, divided, plus more if needed
Nonstick cooking spray
1 cup water
¾ cup confectioners' sugar
1 teaspoon Grand Marnier or other orange liqueur

1. In a large bowl, beat together the butter and sugar with a hand mixer until light and creamy, about 2 minutes. Add the vanilla and orange zest, and beat until combined. Add the eggs one at a time, beating after each addition.
2. In a small bowl, whisk together the flour, baking powder, baking soda, and salt. Add half of the flour mixture to the butter mixture, and beat on low speed until combined. Add the yogurt and beat just until combined. Add the remaining flour mixture and beat until combined. Then add 2 tablespoons of orange juice and beat until combined.
3. Spray a 7-inch (4-cup) Bundt pan with cooking spray. Pour in the batter. Tap the pan lightly on the counter to release any air bubbles, and cover the pan with aluminum foil.

4. Pour the water into the inner pot and insert the trivet. Place the pan on the trivet. Secure the lid.
5. Select Pressure Cook or Manual, adjust the pressure to High, and set the time to 30 minutes. When cooking is complete, let the pressure release naturally for 15 minutes, then quick-release any remaining pressure. Unlock and remove the lid.
6. Carefully remove the pan, then remove the foil. Let the cake cool completely, about 30 minutes. Place a plate over the Bundt pan and invert, shaking gently to release the cake.
7. For the glaze, sift the confectioners' sugar into a small bowl. Whisk in the remaining 1 tablespoon of orange juice and Grand Marnier, adding orange juice as necessary to get a pourable consistency. Drizzle over the cooled cake.

TIP: Using a Bundt or other tube pan ensures that the cake cooks evenly, without an underdone center. If you use a regular cake pan, you may have to adjust the timing.

CARROT-ZUCCHINI CAKE

SERVES 6 | PREP PLUS COOLING TIME: 45 MINUTES | PRESSURE COOK: 30 MINUTES, HIGH
RELEASE: NATURAL FOR 10 MINUTES, THEN QUICK | TOTAL TIME: 1 HOUR 40 MINUTES

Carrot cake has been made and served in North America since colonial times and probably traces its origins back to medieval steamed puddings studded with carrots and bound with eggs and flour. This version skips the addition of raisins and nuts but adds zucchini for moistness.

FOR THE CAKE

1 cup all-purpose flour, plus more for
 coating
½ teaspoon baking soda
1½ teaspoons baking powder
⅛ teaspoon fine salt
1 teaspoon ground cinnamon
½ teaspoon ground nutmeg
½ teaspoon ground ginger

1 cup granulated sugar
½ cup canola oil
¼ cup freshly squeezed orange juice
2 large eggs
¾ cup finely grated carrots
½ cup finely grated zucchini
Nonstick cooking spray
1 cup water

FOR THE FROSTING

¼ cup heavy whipping cream
6 ounces cream cheese, at room
 temperature
½ cup confectioners' sugar

⅛ teaspoon grated orange zest
 (optional)
½ teaspoon pure vanilla extract

1. **MAKE THE CAKE:** In a medium bowl, whisk together the flour, baking soda, baking powder, salt, cinnamon, nutmeg, and ginger. In a large bowl, whisk together the sugar, oil, and orange juice. Add the eggs, and mix thoroughly. Add the flour mixture to the wet mixture, and stir until blended. Stir in the carrots and zucchini.
2. Spray a 7-inch cake pan with cooking spray, and coat with a thin layer of flour. Pour the batter into the pan, and cover with aluminum foil.
3. Pour the water into the inner pot and insert the trivet. Place the pan on the trivet. Secure the lid.

4. Select Pressure Cook or Manual, adjust the pressure to High, and set the time to 30 minutes. When cooking is complete, let the pressure release naturally for 10 minutes, then quick-release any remaining pressure. Unlock and remove the lid.

5. Remove the pan, then remove the foil. Let the cake cool completely, about 30 minutes, then remove it from the pan.

6. **MAKE THE FROSTING:** While the cake is cooling, pour the cream into a small, deep bowl. Using a hand mixer on high speed, whip the cream to form medium-stiff peaks. Set aside. In a large bowl, use the hand mixer to beat the cream cheese until smooth. Add the sugar, orange zest (if using), and vanilla, and beat on low speed until smooth.

7. Scoop about a third of the whipped cream onto the top of the cream cheese mixture. Gently fold it in with a flexible spatula. When the cream is incorporated into the cream cheese mixture, repeat with another third of the whipped cream. Once incorporated, finish with the remaining whipped cream. Top the cooled cake with the frosting.

TIP: Vary the proportions of zucchini and carrots, if you like. You can use all carrots if you don't have or don't like zucchini. If you decrease the amount of carrots (and increase zucchini), you may want to increase the sugar because zucchini isn't as sweet as carrots.

PIES AND FRUIT DESSERTS

LEMON BARS

SERVES 6 | PREP TIME: 15 MINUTES | PRESSURE COOK: 12 MINUTES, HIGH

RELEASE: NATURAL FOR 15 MINUTES, THEN QUICK | TOTAL TIME: 50 MINUTES, PLUS 2 HOURS TO CHILL

The lemon custard in this vegan version of the classic dessert is pleasantly tart; the honey adds a bonus layer of flavor. Most of the tart flavor in these bars comes from the natural oils in the lemon zest, so be sure to include it.

Nonstick cooking spray
¾ cup gluten-free rolled oats
¾ cup almond flour
¼ cup melted coconut oil
2 tablespoons honey, plus ⅓ cup
1 teaspoon pure vanilla extract
¼ teaspoon fine salt, divided

2 large eggs, beaten
Grated zest and juice of 2 lemons
1 teaspoon arrowroot powder
   or cornstarch
1 cup water
Lemon slices, for garnishing (optional)

1. Line a 7-inch round cake pan with aluminum foil, and spray with cooking spray.
2. In a medium bowl, combine the oats, almond flour, coconut oil, 2 tablespoons of honey, vanilla, and ⅛ teaspoon of salt to form a stiff dough. Press the dough into the bottom of the prepared pan.
3. In a separate bowl, whisk together the eggs, lemon zest and juice, arrowroot powder, remaining ⅓ cup of honey, and remaining ⅛ teaspoon of salt. Pour the mixture over the dough. Cover the pan with aluminum foil.
4. Pour the water into the inner pot and insert the trivet. Place the pan on the trivet. Secure the lid.
5. Select Pressure Cook or Manual, adjust the pressure to High, and set the time to 12 minutes. When cooking is complete, let the pressure release naturally for 15 minutes, and then quick-release any remaining pressure. Unlock and remove the lid.
6. Carefully lift out the pan and let cool. Chill the lemon bars in the refrigerator for at least 2 hours before slicing them into 6 portions, garnishing with lemon slices (if using), and serving.

APPLE-PEAR CRUMBLE

SERVES 4 | PREP TIME: 10 MINUTES | PRESSURE COOK: 5 MINUTES, HIGH | RELEASE: QUICK
SAUTÉ: 4 MINUTES | TOTAL TIME: 30 MINUTES

Between the goodness of whole oats and the natural sweetness and sneaky servings of vitamins and minerals in the pears and apples, this delectable dessert is practically good for you. Be sure to serve it warm with vanilla ice cream for a dose of decadence.

3 tablespoons butter, melted
½ cup packed brown sugar
½ cup all-purpose flour
½ cup old-fashioned rolled oats
1 teaspoon ground cinnamon
½ teaspoon freshly grated nutmeg

2 Gala apples, peeled, cored, and sliced (about 2½ cups)
2 Asian pears, peeled, cored, and sliced (about 2½ cups)
½ cup water
Vanilla ice cream, for serving

1. In a small bowl, mix together the butter, brown sugar, flour, oats, cinnamon, and nutmeg.
2. In the inner pot, evenly layer the apples and pears. Evenly spread the oat mixture on top of the fruit. Pour the water on top of the oat mixture. Secure the lid.
3. Select Pressure Cook or Manual, adjust the pressure to High, and set the time to 5 minutes. When cooking is complete, quick-release the pressure. Unlock and remove the lid.
4. Select Sauté, adjust the heat to Medium, and stir the crumble. Let it cook for 3 to 4 minutes, until the sauce thickens. Select Cancel.
5. Serve warm with vanilla ice cream.

TIP: Stir a scoop of this crumble into your oatmeal for an unforgettable breakfast.

PEACH AND BLUEBERRY COBBLER

SERVES 4 TO 6 | PREP PLUS COOLING TIME: 10 MINUTES | PRESSURE COOK: 10 MINUTES, HIGH
RELEASE: NATURAL FOR 18 MINUTES | SAUTÉ: 3 MINUTES | TOTAL TIME: 35 MINUTES

Also known as a "grunt" (because of the sound the bubbling fruit makes when baking) or a "slump" (because of what the cobbler does when placed on a plate), this steamed fruit cobbler is easy to make and ready in record time in the Instant Pot. Top the warm cobbler with freshly whipped cream or vanilla ice cream.

1 cup all-purpose flour
1 tablespoon granulated sugar,
   plus ⅓ cup
1½ teaspoons baking powder
½ teaspoon fine salt
¼ teaspoon baking soda
2 tablespoons cold butter, cubed
⅓ cup buttermilk or whole milk

2 cups peeled, sliced frozen peaches
2 cups frozen blueberries
⅓ cup water
1 tablespoon cornstarch
1 teaspoon freshly squeezed lemon juice
   or lime juice
Pinch ground nutmeg

1. In a medium bowl, mix together the flour, 1 tablespoon of sugar, baking powder, salt, and baking soda until well combined. Add the butter and, using your hands, work it into the flour mixture until it resembles a coarse meal. Add the buttermilk and mix just until moistened. Quickly form a shaggy ball of dough and set aside.
2. Select Sauté and adjust the heat to Low. In the inner pot, combine the peaches, blueberries, water, remaining ⅓ cup of sugar, cornstarch, lemon juice, and nutmeg, and stir for 2 to 3 minutes, until the fruit is defrosted and releases some juice. Select Cancel.
3. Tear off 1-inch balls of the dough and nestle them on top of the fruit, evenly spaced in one layer. (You should have 8 balls.) Secure the lid.
4. Select Manual or Pressure Cook, adjust the pressure to High, and set the time to 10 minutes. When cooking is complete, let the pressure release naturally. Unlock and remove the lid.
5. Let the cobbler cool for a few minutes; the liquid will thicken as it sits. Serve warm.

TANGY KEY LIME PIE

SERVES 4 | PREP PLUS COOLING TIME: 45 MINUTES | PRESSURE COOK: 15 MINUTES, HIGH
RELEASE: NATURAL FOR 18 MINUTES | TOTAL TIME: 1 HOUR 20 MINUTES, PLUS 4 HOURS TO CHILL

This tangy tropical pie tastes like it's made in a thatched hut on a beach rather than in your Instant Pot in your kitchen. If you can't find key limes, regular (Persian) limes work fine.

1 cup water
3 tablespoons unsalted butter, melted, divided
½ cup graham cracker crumbs (from about 4 crackers)
½ teaspoon granulated sugar
2 egg yolks

½ (7-ounce) can sweetened condensed milk
1 tablespoon grated key lime zest
½ cup freshly squeezed key lime juice (from about 12 key limes)
¼ cup sour cream
Whipped cream, for serving

1. Pour the water into the inner pot and insert the trivet. Grease 1 (6-inch) springform pan or 2 (4-inch) springform pans with 1 tablespoon of butter.
2. In a medium bowl, combine the graham cracker crumbs, the remaining 2 tablespoons of butter, and the sugar. Press the crumb mixture evenly into the bottom and up the sides of the prepared pan(s). Refrigerate the crust while you make the filling.
3. In a medium bowl, beat the egg yolks until they thicken and turn pale yellow, 2 to 3 minutes. Gradually beat in the condensed milk until thickened. Slowly add the lime zest and juice, and beat until smooth. Stir in the sour cream.
4. Pour the batter into the prepared pan(s) and cover with aluminum foil. Place the pan(s) on the trivet. Secure the lid.
5. Select Pressure Cook or Manual, adjust the pressure to High, and set the time to 15 minutes. When cooking is complete, allow the pressure to naturally release. Unlock and remove the lid.
6. Using the handles, carefully transfer the trivet and pan to a cooling rack. Remove the foil. When the pie is cool, after about 20 minutes, cover with plastic wrap and refrigerate for at least 4 hours, until set. Serve with whipped cream.

PEACH DUMPLINGS

SERVES 2 TO 4 | PREP PLUS COOLING TIME: 20 MINUTES | PRESSURE COOK 10 MINUTES, HIGH
RELEASE: NATURAL FOR 18 MINUTES | SAUTÉ: 3 MINUTES | TOTAL TIME: 50 MINUTES

Apples always get top billing when it comes to dumpling desserts, but sweet summer peaches deserve their time to shine. Canned crescent rolls, available at your local grocery store, serve as the dumpling pastry in this easy recipe, hugging the peach slices in a buttery, sugary pool of your favorite white wine or rosé.

1 (4-ounce) can crescent rolls
1 tablespoon packed brown sugar,
   plus ¼ cup
1 large peach, peeled, pitted, and cut
   into 4 wedges
2 tablespoons butter

½ teaspoon pure vanilla extract
½ teaspoon ground cinnamon
Pinch ground cardamom
½ cup white wine or rosé (see Tip)
Vanilla ice cream, for serving
Mint sprigs (optional), for serving

1. Remove the crescent rolls from the can and roll them out flat on a cutting board. Sprinkle 1 tablespoon of brown sugar over the surface of the 4 triangles of dough. Roll each peach wedge in a crescent roll.
2. Select Sauté and adjust the heat to Low. Put the butter in the inner pot and let it melt. Add the remaining ¼ cup of brown sugar and the vanilla, cinnamon, and cardamom, and stir until dissolved and combined, about 3 minutes. Select Cancel.
3. Place the peach dumplings side by side in the inner pot. Pour the wine around them. Secure the lid.
4. Select Pressure Cook or Manual, adjust the pressure to High, and set the time to 10 minutes. When cooking is complete, allow the pressure to naturally release. Unlock and remove the lid.
5. Let the dumplings cool for 5 to 8 minutes, then transfer them to serving bowls and place a scoop of vanilla ice cream on the side of each. Drizzle the sweet wine on top, and garnish each with a mint sprig (if desired).

TIP: Choose a light, fruity wine for this dish. Riesling would work well; so would a rosé from Provence in France.

BRANDY-SOAKED CHERRY CHEATER PIE

SERVES 6 TO 8 | PREP PLUS SOAKING TIME: 45 MINUTES | SAUTÉ: 15 MINUTES | TOTAL TIME: 1 HOUR

If you're a fan of pie but not a fan of making pie dough, you'll love these tiny cherry pies. And who's to say you're cheating? No one will ever know. In this recipe, the filling is easy, and by combining delicious cherries with phyllo shells from the freezer section of the grocery store, you'll have a delicious cherry dessert in no time.

2 pounds cherries, pitted
⅓ cup brandy
⅔ cup granulated sugar
3 tablespoons cornstarch

Pinch fine salt
Juice of ½ lime
2 (1.9-ounce) boxes mini phyllo shells, at room temperature

1. In a large bowl, combine the cherries and brandy. Let soak for 30 minutes, stirring occasionally.
2. Select Sauté and adjust the heat to Low. When the display reads "Hot," pour the cherries and whatever liquid is at the bottom of the bowl into the inner pot. Stir in the sugar, cornstarch, salt, and lime juice. Cook for 10 to 15 minutes, stirring frequently so nothing burns, until thickened. Select Cancel.
3. Let cool for a few minutes before spooning the filling into the phyllo shells.

TIP: Frozen cherries are fine to use; thaw them completely before soaking.

WHITE WINE-POACHED PEARS WITH VANILLA

SERVES 6 | PREP TIME: 10 MINUTES | PRESSURE COOK: 8 MINUTES, HIGH | RELEASE: NATURAL FOR 18 MINUTES | SAUTÉ: 10 MINUTES | TOTAL TIME: 50 MINUTES, PLUS OVERNIGHT TO CHILL

Poached pears are an easy but impressive dessert that you can prepare up to two days in advance. Time only enhances the flavor. This recipe uses lighter and fruitier white wine along with vanilla bean and spices to flavor the pears. Serve warm, cold, or at room temperature with a scoop of vanilla ice cream.

1 bottle white wine, such as medium-dry Riesling or Gewürztraminer

1½ cups granulated sugar

6 firm but ripe pears (Bosc or Bartlett), peeled

½ cinnamon stick

2 whole cloves

1 large vanilla bean pod, split open lengthwise

½ lemon, cut into rounds

1. In the inner pot, combine the wine and sugar, and stir until dissolved. Add the pears, cinnamon stick, cloves, vanilla bean pod, and lemon. Secure the lid.
2. Select Pressure Cook or Manual, adjust the pressure to High, and set the time to 8 minutes. When cooking is complete, let the pressure release naturally. Unlock and remove the lid.
3. For best results, refrigerate the pears in their cooking liquid in the inner pot overnight. Let them come to room temperature before proceeding.
4. Remove the pears from the pot and set aside. Discard the cinnamon stick and cloves. Also discard all but 2 cups of the poaching liquid. Select Sauté and adjust the heat to High. Bring the liquid to a boil, and cook the sauce until reduced by half, 5 to 10 minutes. Select Cancel.
5. Serve the pears drizzled with the sauce.

TIP: Poached pears are often cooked in red wine (something light, such as a Beaujolais), so switch out the wine if you like. You may want to add another ½ cup sugar to make up for the difference between the red and white wine.

CITRUS CUSTARD TARTLETS

SERVES 4 | PREP PLUS COOLING TIME: 30 MINUTES | PRESSURE COOK: 6 MINUTES, LOW
RELEASE: NATURAL FOR 10 MINUTES, THEN QUICK | TOTAL TIME: 50 MINUTES, PLUS 2 HOURS TO CHILL

I got the idea for these easy and mouthwatering little desserts from a *New York Times* recipe for a full-size custard tart. Swapping in a crumb crust for the pastry dough, making them tartlet size, and cooking them in the Instant Pot simplified and shortened the time-consuming original recipe.

FOR THE CRUST

⅔ cup vanilla wafer cookie crumbs or graham cracker crumbs (from 10 to 12 wafers or 4 to 5 graham crackers)

3 tablespoons butter, melted, plus more at room temperature for greasing

FOR THE FILLING

4 large eggs
1 cup granulated sugar
2 teaspoons finely grated orange zest
1 teaspoon finely grated lemon zest

½ cup freshly squeezed orange juice
½ cup freshly squeezed lemon juice
¼ cup heavy cream
1 cup water

1. **MAKE THE CRUST:** In a small bowl, mix the cookie crumbs with the 3 tablespoons of melted butter. Grease 4 (1-cup) ramekins or custard cups with butter, and scoop about 3 tablespoons of the crumb mixture into each. Press the crumbs into the bottom of the ramekins.
2. **MAKE THE FILLING:** In a small bowl, whisk together the eggs and sugar. Add the orange zest, lemon zest, orange juice, lemon juice, and cream, and whisk until smooth. Pour the custard evenly into the ramekins.
3. Pour the water into the inner pot and insert the trivet. Arrange the ramekins on the trivet, stacking as necessary. Lay a piece of aluminum foil over the ramekins to keep condensation off the top of the custards. Secure the lid.

4. Select Pressure Cook or Manual, adjust the pressure to Low, and set the time to 6 minutes. When cooking is complete, let the pressure release naturally for 10 minutes, then quick-release any remaining pressure. Unlock and remove the lid.
5. Carefully remove the foil, then use tongs to remove the ramekins from the Instant Pot. Let the custards cool at room temperature for 20 minutes, then refrigerate until chilled, about 2 hours.

TIP: Use a rasp-style grater to remove the zest from the orange and lemon.

BAKED CARAMEL APPLES

SERVES 4 | PREP TIME: 15 MINUTES | PRESSURE COOK: 10 MINUTES, HIGH
RELEASE: NATURAL FOR 18 MINUTES | TOTAL TIME: 45 MINUTES

Apples hold up well in a pressure cooker and, when filled with caramel and toasted nuts, make an impressive afternoon snack or evening treat reminiscent of changing leaves and jack-o'-lanterns. Top with vanilla ice cream to take it to the next level.

4 Granny Smith apples
¼ cup Chocolate-Caramel Sauce
   (page 86) or store-bought
   caramel sauce

2 tablespoons chopped roasted almonds
1 cup water
Nonstick cooking spray

1. Using a paring knife, cut around the stem of the apples and down around the core. Scoop out the stem and seeds, leaving the bottom of each apple intact.
2. In a small bowl, combine the caramel sauce and almonds. Fill the apples with the mixture.
3. Pour the water into the inner pot. Spray the trivet with cooking spray and insert it in the pot. Place the apples on the prepared trivet. Secure the lid.
4. Select Pressure Cook or Manual, set the pressure to High, and set the time to 10 minutes. When cooking is complete, let the pressure release naturally. Unlock and remove the lid.
5. Carefully remove the trivet and the apples, and serve warm.

TIP: You can also fill the apples with a combination of raisins, chopped walnuts, a sprinkling of lemon or orange zest, and brown sugar for a streusel version.

STRAWBERRIES ROMANOFF

**SERVES 4 | PREP PLUS COOLING TIME: 40 MINUTES | PRESSURE COOK: 2 MINUTES, LOW
RELEASE: NATURAL FOR 10 MINUTES, THEN QUICK | TOTAL TIME: 1 HOUR**

At its simplest, strawberries Romanoff is just a bowl of tiny wild strawberries served with crème fraîche and brown sugar. In this version, making a sauce from some of the berries intensifies their flavor, a welcome boost when using supermarket berries.

3 pints fresh strawberries, divided
2 tablespoons orange liqueur, such as
   Grand Marnier or curaçao
½ cup packed light brown sugar, divided,
   plus more for serving, if desired

½ cup heavy cream
2 tablespoons sour cream or crème
   fraîche

1. Remove the stems from the strawberries, and cut into quarters if large or halves if small.
2. Put one-third of the berries in the inner pot. Stir in the orange liqueur and ¼ cup of brown sugar. Let sit for about 10 minutes, or until the berries start to release their juices. Stir again, and secure the lid.
3. Select Pressure Cook or Manual, adjust the pressure to Low, and set the time to 2 minutes. When cooking is complete, let the pressure release naturally for 10 minutes, then quick-release any remaining pressure. Unlock and remove the lid.
4. Using a potato masher or large fork, mash the berries to a thick consistency, not completely smooth. Transfer the berry mixture to a large bowl and let it cool to room temperature, about 20 minutes.
5. Mix the remaining two-thirds of the strawberries into the sauce. Stir in 3 tablespoons of brown sugar, and set aside.
6. In a medium bowl, whip the heavy cream with the remaining 1 tablespoon of brown sugar until medium-stiff peaks form. Fold in the sour cream.
7. To serve, spoon the berries into bowls and top with a big spoonful of the whipped cream. Sprinkle with additional brown sugar, if desired.

RICOTTA RASPBERRY CUPS

SERVES 4 | PREP PLUS COOLING TIME: 30 MINUTES | PRESSURE COOK: 6 MINUTES, HIGH
RELEASE: NATURAL FOR 8 MINUTES, THEN QUICK | TOTAL TIME: 50 MINUTES, PLUS 3 HOURS TO CHILL

A refreshing change of pace from traditional cheesecake, these ricotta cups are creamy and filled with raspberries. They make a delightful summer dessert when berries are in season, but you can also use frozen berries. If you do, the raspberries that go into the batter should be frozen, but the raspberries that top the finished cups should be thawed.

4 ounces cream cheese
¼ cup heavy cream
⅓ cup Homemade Ricotta Cheese
(page 93) or store-bought whole-milk
ricotta cheese
⅓ cup granulated sugar, plus
1 tablespoon

1 teaspoon pure vanilla extract
1 egg
1 egg yolk
1 cup fresh raspberries, divided
Nonstick cooking spray
1 cup water

1. In a small bowl, combine the cream cheese and heavy cream, and beat until smooth with a hand mixer. Add the ricotta, ⅓ cup of sugar, and the vanilla, and beat until the mixture is smooth again.
2. Beat in the egg and the egg yolk until fully incorporated. Gently stir in ½ cup of raspberries.
3. Generously spray 4 (6-ounce) ramekins with cooking spray. Divide the cheesecake batter among the ramekins.
4. Pour the water into the inner pot and insert the trivet. Arrange the ramekins on the trivet, stacking carefully if needed. Lay a piece of aluminum foil over the ramekins (but don't crimp it down). Secure the lid.
5. Select Pressure Cook or Manual, adjust the pressure to High, and set the time to 6 minutes. When cooking is complete, let the pressure release naturally for 8 minutes, then quick-release any remaining pressure. Unlock and remove the lid.

6. Use tongs to remove the ramekins. Let cool for 20 minutes or so, then refrigerate to chill thoroughly, 3 to 4 hours.

7. Prepare the topping. In a small bowl, stir together the remaining 1 tablespoon of sugar and remaining ½ cup of raspberries, mashing lightly to release some of the juices from the berries.

8. When ready to serve, run a knife around the inside of each ramekin. Unmold by placing a plate over each ramekin and turning upside down so the cheesecake pops out (or, if you prefer, leave the cakes in the ramekins). Serve with the raspberry topping

TIP: If you enjoy making your own ricotta cheese, this is the perfect place to use it, but if not, store-bought ricotta works fine. Just be sure to buy whole-milk and not skim or part-skim ricotta.

FROZEN "CREAMSICLE" MOUSSE

SERVES 8 | PREP TIME: 15 MINUTES | PRESSURE COOK: 10 MINUTES, HIGH | RELEASE: NATURAL FOR 10 MINUTES, THEN QUICK | TOTAL TIME: 40 MINUTES, PLUS 2 HOURS TO CHILL AND 4 HOURS TO FREEZE

If you were one of those kids running after the ice cream truck every summer to make sure you didn't miss out on your Creamsicle push-up pop, this dessert is made for you. The combination of orange curd and vanilla-flavored whipped cream makes a simple but impressive frozen treat just filled with long-summer-day nostalgia.

½ cup granulated sugar
4 tablespoons butter, at room temperature
4 large egg yolks
⅓ cup orange juice concentrate, plus 1 teaspoon

2 teaspoons grated orange zest
Pinch fine salt
1 cup water
½ cup heavy cream, very cold
1 teaspoon pure vanilla extract

1. In a 1-quart soufflé dish or bowl (6 to 7 inches in diameter), beat the sugar and butter with a hand mixer until the sugar has mostly dissolved and the mixture is light-colored and fluffy. Add the egg yolks and beat until combined. Add ⅓ cup of orange juice concentrate, the zest, and salt, and beat to combine. The mixture will probably appear grainy, but that's okay. Cover the bowl with aluminum foil.

2. Pour the water into the inner pot and insert the trivet. Place the dish on the trivet. Secure the lid.

3. Select Pressure Cook or Manual, adjust the pressure to High, and set the time to 10 minutes. When cooking is complete, let the pressure release naturally for 10 minutes, then quick-release any remaining pressure. Unlock and remove the lid.

4. Carefully remove the dish and foil. The mixture will appear clumpy and curdled.

5. Whisk the curd mixture until smooth. Place a fine strainer over a medium bowl and pour the curd through it, pressing down with a flexible spatula to pass the curd through, leaving the zest and any curdled egg bits behind. Be sure to scrape any curd on the bottom of the strainer into the bowl. Cover with plastic wrap, pushing the wrap down on top of the curd to keep a skin from forming. Refrigerate until set, 2 to 4 hours.

6. While the orange curd sets, in a medium bowl, combine the cream, vanilla, and remaining 1 teaspoon of orange juice concentrate. Using a hand mixer, whip until soft peaks form.

7. When the orange curd is set, spoon about two-thirds of the whipped cream onto it. Beat on medium-high speed until thoroughly combined. Fold in the remaining whipped cream gently, by hand. Pour the orange cream into ramekins and place in the freezer 4 to 6 hours, until frozen.

TIP: Step it up with a pie version by spooning the orange cream into a homemade or store-bought graham cracker crust and freezing. Garnish with additional whipped cream, and sprinkle with finely grated orange zest.

CHAPTER 5

CUSTARDS AND PUDDINGS

FIVE-STAR FLAN

SERVES 6 | PREP PLUS COOLING TIME: 30 MINUTES | PRESSURE COOK: 8 MINUTES, HIGH

RELEASE: NATURAL FOR 10 MINUTES, THEN QUICK | SAUTÉ: 6 MINUTES

TOTAL TIME: 1 HOUR, PLUS 2 HOURS TO CHILL

Traditionally, flan is cooked in a water bath, but using the Instant Pot produces an extra-smooth custard without the fuss.

½ cup granulated sugar
1 tablespoon water, plus 1 cup
6 large egg yolks
¼ cup whole milk

1 (14-ounce) can sweetened
  condensed milk
1 teaspoon pure vanilla extract
Pinch fine salt

1. Select Sauté and adjust the heat to Medium. In the inner pot, combine the sugar and 1 tablespoon of water, and cook, stirring constantly, until the sugar melts and starts to bubble and it turns dark golden brown, about 5 minutes. Select Cancel.
2. Divide the caramel among 6 ramekins or custard cups and set aside. Wash out the inner pot and return it to the base.
3. In a medium bowl, beat together the egg yolks, whole milk, sweetened condensed milk, vanilla, and salt until thoroughly combined. Pour the custard mixture through a fine-mesh sieve into the caramel-lined rame-kins. Tap them gently on the counter to release any air bubbles. Cover each ramekin tightly with aluminum foil.
4. Pour the water into the inner pot and insert the trivet. Arrange the ramekins on the trivet, stacking if necessary. Secure the lid.
5. Select Pressure Cook or Manual, adjust the pressure to High, and set the time to 8 minutes. When cooking is complete, let the pressure release naturally for 10 minutes, then quick-release any remaining pressure. Unlock and remove the lid.
6. Using tongs, carefully remove the ramekins, then remove the foil. Let the flan cool at room temperature for 20 to 30 minutes, then refrigerate until chilled, about 2 hours.
7. When ready to serve, run a knife around the inside of each ramekin. Place a small plate over each and invert the flan onto it, then scrape out the caramel over the custard.

ESPRESSO POTS DE CRÈME

SERVES 4 | PREP PLUS COOLING TIME: 30 MINUTES | PRESSURE COOK: 6 MINUTES, HIGH

RELEASE: NATURAL FOR 10 MINUTES, THEN QUICK | TOTAL TIME: 50 MINUTES, PLUS 2 HOURS TO CHILL

Hailing from France, pots de crème is a fancy name for individual, extra-rich custards traditionally served in small covered porcelain pots. But you don't need the fancy pots or fluency in French to make this tasty coffee-flavored dessert. It's equally delicious wherever you are and in regular ramekins.

1 egg
3 egg yolks
¾ cup granulated sugar
½ teaspoon pure vanilla extract

1 cup whole milk
1 cup heavy cream
2 tablespoons instant espresso powder
1 cup water

1. In a medium bowl, beat the egg, egg yolks, sugar, and vanilla with a hand mixer until the sugar is dissolved. Add the milk, cream, and espresso powder. Beat briefly to combine. Pour into 4 small ramekins or custard cups. (You may find it easier to do this if you transfer the custard into a measuring cup with a pouring lip.) Cover each ramekin tightly with aluminum foil.

2. Pour the water into the inner pot and insert the trivet. Arrange the ramekins on the trivet, stacking if necessary. Secure the lid.

3. Select Pressure Cook or Manual, adjust the pressure to High, and set the time to 6 minutes. When cooking is complete, let the pressure release naturally for 10 minutes, then quick-release any remaining pressure. Unlock and remove the lid.

4. Using tongs, carefully remove the ramekins, then remove the foil. Let the custards cool at room temperature for 20 minutes, then cover with plastic wrap and refrigerate until chilled, about 2 hours.

TIP: Espresso powder can be found in the coffee section of most grocery stores or purchased online. Italian brands are generally considered the best choice.

DULCE DE LECHE

SERVES 4 | PREP PLUS COOLING TIME: 35 MINUTES | PRESSURE COOK: 45 MINUTES, HIGH
RELEASE: NATURAL FOR 18 MINUTES | TOTAL TIME: 1 HOUR 40 MINUTES

Dulce de leche comes from South America and is a sweet drink sometimes referred to as "caramelized milk." The basic drink contains just two ingredients and requires minimal effort, especially using the Instant Pot. Spoon it over crunchy cookies and top it with chocolate and nuts, and you end up with a candy bar in a bowl.

1 (14-ounce) can sweetened
  condensed milk
2 cups water
½ teaspoon fine salt

8 shortbread cookies, broken into
  several pieces
¼ cup chopped roasted almonds
¼ cup chopped dark chocolate

1. Pour the sweetened condensed milk into a 2-cup measuring cup or other container. Tightly cover with aluminum foil.
2. Pour the water into the inner pot and place the measuring cup inside. The water should come up to about the level of the milk. Secure the lid.
3. Select Pressure Cook or Manual, adjust the pressure to High, and set the time to 45 minutes. When cooking is complete, naturally release the pressure. Unlock and remove the lid.
4. Carefully remove the measuring cup. Remove the foil and stir in the salt. Let cool for 20 to 30 minutes.
5. To serve, divide the cookies among 4 bowls, and add the dulce de leche. Top with the chopped almonds and chocolate.

TIP: Without the cookies, nuts, and chocolate, dulce le leche can be used as a topping for ice cream or cheesecake. It's also delicious over White Wine–Poached Pears with Vanilla (page 59) or Sticky Toffee Pudding (page 81).

LITTLE PUMPKIN PUDDINGS

SERVES 4 | PREP PLUS COOLING TIME: 1 HOUR 5 MINUTES | PRESSURE COOK: 15 MINUTES, HIGH
RELEASE: NATURAL FOR 18 MINUTES | TOTAL TIME: 1 HOUR 40 MINUTES

When you're craving pumpkin pie but don't have the time to make it, don't reach for those pricey pumpkin spice lattes—make these puddings instead. They're so much quicker to whip up and cook than a whole pie, and yet they satisfy all of those pumpkin cravings. These puddings also make a lovely gluten-free Thanksgiving dessert.

1 cup water
1 tablespoon butter, for greasing
1 cup pumpkin puree (not pumpkin pie filling)
¼ cup granulated sugar
½ teaspoon ground cinnamon
¼ teaspoon fine salt

¼ teaspoon ground ginger
Pinch ground cloves
¾ cup half-and-half
1 egg, beaten
1 egg yolk
½ teaspoon pure vanilla extract

1. Pour the water into the inner pot and insert the trivet. Grease 4 (1-cup) ramekins or custard cups with the butter.
2. In a medium bowl, whisk together the pumpkin, sugar, cinnamon, salt, ginger, and cloves until combined. Add the half-and-half, egg, egg yolk, and vanilla. Whisk until creamy.
3. Pour the mixture into the ramekins, dividing evenly. Arrange the ramekins on the trivet, stacking if necessary. Secure the lid.
4. Select Pressure Cook or Manual, adjust the pressure to High, and set the time to 15 minutes. When cooking is complete, naturally release the pressure. Unlock and carefully remove the lid so that water doesn't drip on the top of the puddings.
5. Let the puddings sit until the steam dies down, and then very carefully lift them out. Let them cool to room temperature before serving, 1 to 2 hours.

TIP: Any other 1-cup heatproof containers will work in this recipe, including mugs, baking cups, and small soufflé dishes.

CHOCOLATE AND ORANGE BREAD PUDDING

SERVES 4 OR 5 | PREP TIME: 15 MINUTES | PRESSURE COOK: 15 MINUTES
RELEASE: NATURAL FOR 18 MINUTES | TOTAL TIME: 50 MINUTES

Bread pudding cooks happily in the pressure cooker, with the steam making it extra fluffy. Orange zest, dark chocolate, and almond extract add rich, sophisticated flavors. It's also a tasty way to use up any stale bread you have lying around.

2 cups water

1 teaspoon butter, for greasing

3 large eggs

⅓ cup granulated sugar, plus 1 tablespoon

½ cup whole or 2 percent milk

¾ cup heavy cream or half-and-half

Grated zest of 1 orange

2 tablespoons freshly squeezed orange juice

1 teaspoon almond extract

Pinch table salt

3½ cups (¾-inch cubes) stale French bread

3 ounces high-quality dark or semisweet chocolate, cut into small pieces

1. Pour the water into the inner pot and insert the trivet. Grease a 6- to 7-inch soufflé or baking dish with the butter.
2. In a large bowl, whisk together the eggs and ⅓ cup of sugar until well mixed. Add the milk, cream, orange zest and juice, almond extract, and salt. Mix well.
3. Add the bread and toss until all the cubes are coated. Let sit for 5 minutes, stirring once or twice.
4. Add the chocolate and mix. Pour the mixture into the soufflé dish, pressing down if needed to fit. Sprinkle the top with the remaining 1 tablespoon of sugar. Place the dish on the trivet. Secure the lid.
5. Select Pressure Cook or Manual, adjust the pressure to High, and set the time to 15 minutes. When cooking is complete, naturally release the pressure. Unlock and remove the lid carefully and quickly so that condensation doesn't drip on the pudding.
6. Carefully remove the dish, and serve warm.

MOLTEN BROWNIE PUDDING

SERVES 3 OR 4 | PREP PLUS COOLING TIME: 15 MINUTES | PRESSURE COOK: 30 MINUTES, HIGH
RELEASE: QUICK | TOTAL TIME: 1 HOUR

Totally decadent, this exceptional dessert is for all the chocolate lovers out there. Once cooked, the pudding is creamy, buttery, and rich, with all the flavors of a good brownie. Serve with a scoop of vanilla ice cream.

1½ cups water
7 tablespoons butter, melted, divided
1 cup granulated sugar
2 eggs
¼ cup all-purpose flour
¼ cup plus 2 tablespoons unsweetened
   cocoa powder

Pinch table salt
½ teaspoon pure vanilla extract
¼ cup semisweet chocolate chips
Vanilla ice cream, for serving

1. Pour the water into the inner pot and insert the trivet. Grease a 6- to 7-inch soufflé or baking dish with 1 tablespoon of butter.
2. In a large bowl, use a hand mixer to beat together the sugar and eggs until light yellow and fluffy, 3 to 5 minutes.
3. In a small bowl, combine the flour, cocoa powder, and salt, and whisk until no lumps remain. Add the dry ingredients to the sugar-and-egg mixture, and mix just until combined. Add the vanilla and the remaining 6 tablespoons of butter, and mix until just combined.
4. Pour the mixture into the prepared soufflé dish, and top with the chocolate chips. Place the dish on the trivet. Secure the lid.
5. Select Pressure Cook or Manual, adjust the pressure to High, and set the time to 30 minutes. When cooking is complete, quick-release the pressure. Unlock and carefully remove the lid so that any condensation doesn't drip on the pudding.
6. Using oven mitts, carefully remove the dish. Let cool for at least 5 minutes before serving with vanilla ice cream.

TIP: Instead of chocolate chips, try topping the pudding with peanut butter chips or butterscotch chips.

COCONUT-ALMOND RICE PUDDING

SERVES 2 | PREP TIME: 5 MINUTES | PRESSURE COOK: 12 MINUTES, HIGH
RELEASE: NATURAL FOR 10 MINUTES | SAUTÉ: 10 MINUTES | TOTAL TIME: 40 MINUTES

This recipe was inspired by a Norwegian Christmas Eve tradition. Before feasting on fiskeboller (fish balls) and potatoes with gravy, families eat through a big pot of rice pudding until someone finds a single boiled almond, signifying a year of good luck. Although coconut milk isn't traditionally used in the pudding, it adds a creaminess that is irresistible.

1 tablespoon butter
½ cup arborio rice
1 cup coconut milk (from a can), divided
¼ cup water
¼ cup granulated sugar

½ teaspoon almond extract
¼ teaspoon ground cinnamon
Pinch kosher salt
Sliced roasted almonds, for serving
Shredded coconut, for serving

1. Select Sauté and adjust the heat to Low. Put the butter in the inner pot to melt. Add the rice and sauté for 1 minute, stirring. Add ½ cup of coconut milk, the water, sugar, almond extract, cinnamon, and salt. Simmer for 1 to 2 minutes to dissolve the sugar. Select Cancel. Secure the lid.
2. Select Pressure Cook or Manual, adjust the pressure to High, and set the time to 12 minutes. When cooking is complete, let the pressure release naturally.
3. Select Sauté again and adjust the heat to Low. Stir the pudding, then add the remaining ½ cup of coconut milk, stirring until it reaches the desired texture, about 5 minutes. Select Cancel.
4. Divide between 2 bowls and garnish with almonds and shredded coconut.

TIP: To lower the calorie count but maintain the coconut flavor, reduce the amount of coconut milk and use coconut water instead, making sure to still use 1 cup total.

FRENCH VANILLA YOGURT CUSTARD

SERVES 4 | PREP PLUS COOLING TIME: 40 MINUTES | PRESSURE COOK: 25 MINUTES, HIGH
RELEASE: NATURAL FOR 18 MINUTES | TOTAL TIME: 1 HOUR 30 MINUTES, PLUS 3 HOURS TO CHILL

NUT-FREE

5-INGREDIENT

The term "French vanilla" comes from the classic French method for making ice cream with an egg-based custard, which gives it a richer texture and deeper flavor than vanilla alone. Using yogurt instead of milk or cream makes this custard delightfully tangy. With just a handful of ingredients, it's as easy as it is delicious.

1 cup European or Greek Yogurt
   (page 90) or store-bought plain
   Greek yogurt
1 cup sweetened condensed milk

2 egg yolks
1½ teaspoons pure vanilla extract
1 cup water

1. In a heatproof bowl that fits inside the Instant Pot, mix together the yogurt, condensed milk, egg yolks, and vanilla. Tightly cover the bowl with aluminum foil.
2. Pour the water into the inner pot and insert the trivet. Place the bowl on the trivet. Secure the lid.
3. Select Pressure Cook or Manual, adjust the pressure to High, and set the time to 25 minutes. When cooking is complete, naturally release the pressure. Unlock and remove the lid.
4. Carefully remove the bowl. Let the custard cool for 30 minutes, then refrigerate, covered, for 3 to 4 hours before serving.

TIP: Serve with fresh fruit, Mixed Berry Compote (page 84), or Blueberry-Peach Sauce (page 88).

TAPIOCA PUDDING

SERVES 4 | PREP PLUS COOLING TIME: 10 MINUTES | PRESSURE COOK: 6 MINUTES, HIGH
RELEASE: NATURAL FOR 18 MINUTES | TOTAL TIME: 35 MINUTES

Tapioca is a starch extracted from the cassava plant. It's available as a flour or as "pearls" of various sizes. You'll sometimes see the pearls used in super-trendy bubble tea. The pearls soften when cooked and, mixed with milk and egg, turn into a delicious dessert similar to rice pudding. It can be served warm or cold.

3 cups water
1 cup medium tapioca pearls
2 cups whole milk
½ cup granulated sugar

1 large egg
1 tablespoon pure vanilla extract
½ teaspoon fine salt

1. In the inner pot, combine the water and tapioca pearls. Secure the lid.
2. Select Pressure Cook or Manual, adjust the pressure to High, and set the time to 6 minutes. When cooking is complete, naturally release the pressure. Unlock and remove the lid.
3. Stir in the milk, sugar, egg, vanilla, and salt while the tapioca is still piping hot. Let it cool for a few minutes before serving, or if you prefer it cold, chill it in the refrigerator for 1 to 2 hours.

TIP: Bob's Red Mill medium tapioca pearls are a good choice for this recipe.

STICKY TOFFEE PUDDING

SERVES 2 | PREP PLUS COOLING TIME: 30 MINUTES | PRESSURE COOK: 25 MINUTES, HIGH
RELEASE: QUICK | TOTAL TIME: 1 HOUR 10 MINUTES

Dense and moist, this sticky toffee pudding is studded with dates. If you have the time, use Chocolate-Caramel Sauce (page 86) or Dulce de Leche (page 73). If not, just choose your favorite store-bought sauce. Either way, this British classic will soon become a favorite.

1 cup water
1½ teaspoons unsalted butter, at room temperature, divided
¼ cup Medjool dates, pitted and chopped
½ cup boiling water
½ cup all-purpose flour
1 egg

½ teaspoon baking soda
Pinch kosher salt
1 tablespoon molasses
¼ cup plus 2 tablespoons packed dark brown sugar
½ teaspoon pure vanilla extract
Caramel or toffee sauce, for serving

1. Pour the water into the inner pot, and insert the trivet. Grease 2 (1-cup) ramekins with 1 teaspoon of butter, and set aside.
2. In a small bowl, cover the dates with the boiling water to soften them for about 5 minutes. Strain the dates (reserving the water) and let them cool for 10 minutes.
3. In a food processor or blender bowl, combine the flour, egg, baking soda, salt, molasses, brown sugar, and vanilla, and pulse until just combined. Add the softened, cooled dates and ¼ cup of their soaking water, and pulse until almost smooth.
4. Divide the batter evenly between the 2 prepared ramekins. Cover each with a piece of foil greased with the remaining ½ teaspoon of butter, sealing tightly. Set the ramekins on the trivet. Secure the lid.
5. Select Pressure Cook or Manual, adjust the pressure to High, and set the time to 25 minutes. When cooking is complete, quick-release the pressure. Unlock and remove the lid.
6. Using tongs, carefully remove the ramekins and put them on a cooling rack for 10 minutes.
7. Remove the foil, turn out the puddings onto dessert plates, and serve warm with caramel or toffee sauce.

CHAPTER 6

SAUCES AND STAPLES

MIXED BERRY COMPOTE

MAKES 2 CUPS | PREP TIME: 10 MINUTES | PRESSURE COOK: 2 MINUTES, HIGH
RELEASE: NATURAL FOR 10 MINUTES, THEN QUICK | TOTAL TIME: 30 MINUTES

This compote is a delicious, versatile fruit mixture you can use on breakfasts, such as European or Greek Yogurt (page 90), or desserts, such as Orange Pound Cake (page 46). Because different berries have different sweetness levels, start with a small amount of sugar before cooking and adjust as necessary afterward. The fruits start to release liquid almost immediately when you mix them with sugar, so you won't need to add liquid for the cooking process.

4 cups fresh berries, such as strawberries, raspberries, blueberries, or blackberries

¼ cup granulated sugar, plus more as needed

1 teaspoon freshly squeezed lemon juice

1 teaspoon orange juice concentrate (optional)

1. If you're using strawberries, remove the stems and cut the berries in halves or quarters, depending on size. Wash all the berries.
2. In the inner pot, combine the berries and sugar. Stir to start dissolving the sugar. Add the lemon juice and orange juice concentrate (if using). Secure the lid.
3. Select Pressure Cook or Manual, adjust the pressure to High, and set the time to 2 minutes. When cooking is complete, let the pressure release naturally for 10 minutes, then quick-release any remaining pressure. Unlock and remove the lid.
4. Taste the berries (carefully—they're hot) and adjust the sugar. The berries will be soupy but will thicken up slightly as they cool.

TIP: If you prefer a thicker compote, you can strain off some of the juice and mix the strained juice into sparkling water for a super refreshing drink.

LEMON CURD

MAKES 2 CUPS | PREP TIME: 10 MINUTES | PRESSURE COOK: 10 MINUTES, HIGH
RELEASE: NATURAL FOR 10 MINUTES, THEN QUICK | TOTAL TIME: 40 MINUTES, PLUS 2 HOURS TO CHILL

Lemon curd, essentially a tangy lemon custard, is a standard on scones at British high teas, but it's also excellent stirred into European or Greek Yogurt (page 90) or atop Fruity Cheesecake with Chocolate Cookie Crust (page 33). Lightened with some whipped cream, it also makes an amazing lemon mousse.

¾ cup granulated sugar
5 tablespoons butter, at room
   temperature
Grated zest of 1 lemon
1 cup freshly squeezed lemon juice (from
   4 to 5 lemons)

3 large eggs
2 large egg yolks
1 cup water

1. In a medium bowl, blend the sugar, butter, and lemon zest together with a hand mixer. Beat in the lemon juice, whole eggs, and egg yolks, and mix well. The mixture won't be completely smooth. Transfer the mixture to a 7-inch glass bowl and cover it with foil.
2. Pour the water into the inner pot and insert the trivet. Lower the bowl onto the trivet. Secure the lid.
3. Select Pressure Cook or Manual, adjust the pressure to High, and set the time to 10 minutes. When cooking is complete, allow the pressure to naturally release for 10 minutes, then quick-release any remaining pressure. Unlock and remove the lid.
4. Carefully lift out the bowl and remove the foil. Whisk the curd, then pour it through a fine sieve into another medium bowl. Chill in the refrigerator for 2 hours before serving.

TIP: The lemon curd can last in a sealed container in the refrigerator for up to 2 weeks, or you can freeze it for up to 1 month.

CHOCOLATE-CARAMEL SAUCE

MAKES 2 CUPS | PREP TIME: 20 MINUTES | PRESSURE COOK: 50 MINUTES, HIGH
RELEASE: NATURAL FOR 18 MINUTES | TOTAL TIME: 1 HOUR 40 MINUTES

Anyone who's made caramel the old-fashioned way on the stove knows that it requires constant attention, stirring at the right time, not stirring at the wrong time, and avoiding a boil-over. No more of that! This recipe yields a silky-smooth, perfectly balanced chocolate-caramel sauce that's outstanding as a topping for ice cream or cheesecake or as a spread for sandwich cookies, minus the stove-top frustration.

1 (14-ounce) can sweetened
   condensed milk
Water, as needed
¼ cup heavy whipping cream
1 tablespoon unsalted butter, at room
   temperature

½ teaspoon pure vanilla extract
⅛ teaspoon fine salt
3 ounces bittersweet chocolate,
   chopped

1. Pour the condensed milk into a heatproof 2-cup measuring cup or small bowl that is large enough to fit all of the ingredients. Cover the cup with aluminum foil and crimp the edges over the top. Place the cup in the inner pot, and add enough water to the pot to reach the level of the milk in the cup. Secure the lid.

2. Select Pressure Cook or Manual, adjust the pressure to High, and set the time to 50 minutes. When cooking is complete, naturally release the pressure. Unlock and remove the lid.

3. Lift the cup out of the pot and remove the foil. Add the cream, butter, vanilla, and salt. Use an immersion blender to blend the sauce until it's smooth. While the sauce is still hot, add the chocolate and whisk to melt it into the caramel. Use right away, or refrigerate in an airtight container for several weeks.

TIP: For plain caramel sauce, simply omit the chocolate. For salted caramel sauce, add ¼ teaspoon more salt.

CINNAMON-VANILLA APPLESAUCE

**SERVES 6 TO 8 | PREP TIME: 10 MINUTES | PRESSURE COOK: 5 MINUTES, HIGH
RELEASE: NATURAL FOR 10 MINUTES, THEN QUICK | TOTAL TIME: 30 MINUTES**

Applesauce is delicious enough to feel like a treat yet nutritious enough to be a healthy snack. Stir some into a bowl of granola, or use it in baking, as in Chocolate Chip Banana Bread (page 20). Choose a combination of apples for best results. Fuji and Golden Delicious apples cook down quickly and easily, and Honeycrisp and Granny Smiths add wonderful flavor.

3 pounds apples, cored and quartered
⅓ cup water
1 teaspoon pure vanilla extract
1 teaspoon ground cinnamon, plus more
    as needed

1 teaspoon freshly squeezed lemon juice
½ teaspoon fine salt

1. In the inner pot, combine the apples, water, vanilla, cinnamon, lemon juice, and salt. Secure the lid.
2. Select Pressure Cook or Manual, adjust the pressure to High, and set the time to 5 minutes. When cooking is complete, let the pressure release naturally for 10 minutes, then quick-release any remaining pressure. Unlock and carefully remove the lid.
3. Using an immersion blender, blend the applesauce until smooth. Taste and add more cinnamon, as desired.

TIP: If you like, leave the apple peels on for the extra fiber; there's not very much taste or texture difference after they've been blended.

BLUEBERRY-PEACH SAUCE

SERVES 4 | PREP PLUS COOLING TIME: 30 MINUTES | PRESSURE COOK: 2 MINUTES, HIGH
RELEASE: QUICK | TOTAL TIME: 45 MINUTES

Raw blueberries don't make for a great sauce, but cooked blueberries quickly lose all their texture. The trick is to combine the two so the cooked puree softens the rest of the berries. In this recipe, the peach not only adds a hint of its flavor but also contributes pectin to thicken the sauce.

1 ripe peach, peeled, pitted, and
  chopped
1 teaspoon freshly squeezed lemon juice
1 tablespoon cornstarch

2 tablespoons water
2½ cups fresh blueberries, divided
¼ cup granulated sugar
¼ teaspoon grated lemon zest

1. In a small bowl, use an immersion blender or large fork to puree the peach and lemon juice. In another small bowl or cup, mix the cornstarch with the water.
2. Pour the peach puree into the inner pot. Add 1 cup of blueberries, the cornstarch mixture, the sugar, and the lemon zest. Stir to distribute the cornstarch mixture. Secure the lid.
3. Select Pressure Cook or Manual, adjust the pressure to High, and set the time to 2 minutes. When cooking is complete, quick-release the pressure. Unlock and carefully remove the lid.
4. The berries should be split and very soft. Mash them with a potato masher or large fork. Stir in the remaining 1½ cups of blueberries. Stir to coat with the cooked mixture, and let sit for 10 minutes or so, stirring occasionally, to soften the raw berries slightly. Let the sauce cool for 15 minutes.

TIP: If not using immediately, store the sauce in the refrigerator in a container with a tight-fitting lid for up to 3 days.

GINGER PEAR BUTTER

MAKES 2 CUPS | PREP PLUS COOLING TIME: 1 HOUR 10 MINUTES | PRESSURE COOK: 5 MINUTES, HIGH
RELEASE: NATURAL FOR 8 MINUTES, THEN QUICK | SAUTÉ: 20 MINUTES TO 1 HOUR
TOTAL TIME: 2 TO 2½ HOURS

Like its better-known cousin, apple butter, pear butter is a thick, spicy, sweet condiment perfect for topping or dipping toast, pancakes, or pound cake. Or if you're like me, just eat it by the spoonful.

2 pounds pears (Bosc or Bartlett), peeled, cored, and quartered
4 or 5 slices fresh ginger (each about the size of a quarter)
1 small cinnamon stick

2 tablespoons freshly squeezed lemon juice
¼ cup water
½ cup packed brown sugar, plus more to taste
Pinch fine salt

1. In the inner pot, combine the pears, ginger, cinnamon, lemon juice, and water. Secure the lid.
2. Select Pressure Cook or Manual, adjust the pressure to High, and set the time to 5 minutes. When cooking is complete, let the pressure release naturally for 8 minutes, then quick-release any remaining pressure. Unlock and remove the lid.
3. Remove the ginger slices and cinnamon stick. Use an immersion blender or potato masher to puree the pears. Stir in the brown sugar and salt.
4. Select Sauté and adjust the heat to Low. Simmer the pear mixture, stirring occasionally, until it thickens enough to leave a stripe on the bottom of the pot when you scrape the spoon through the mixture. (You can also spoon a little onto a cold plate; it should not run.) This can take anywhere from 20 minutes to 1 hour, depending on the moisture level of the pears. Taste and adjust the sweetness to your liking. If you add more sugar, let the pear butter simmer until the sugar dissolves.
5. Select Cancel. Let it cool for 1 hour, then transfer it to an airtight container. Store in the refrigerator for up to 2 weeks.

TIP: If you're familiar with water bath canning, this recipe is a great candidate. You can easily double the recipe and preserve it in half-pint jars.

EUROPEAN OR GREEK YOGURT

**MAKES 4 CUPS | PREP TIME: 30 MINUTES | YOGURT: 8 HOURS 25 MINUTES
TOTAL TIME: 9 HOURS, PLUS 4 HOURS TO CHILL**

Making your own yogurt takes some time, but it's mostly unattended, so the process is easy. You have total control over how tangy and thick you want it, and it has no additives. European-style yogurt is a bit thinner and tangier than Greek-style, which is strained before using.

1 quart whole milk
1 tablespoon plain whole-milk
   yogurt with live cultures, at room
   temperature

1. Pour the milk into the inner pot. Select the Yogurt function, and press Adjust so that "Boil" shows in the display. Secure the lid, with the pressure valve set to the "venting" position. When the beeper sounds (between 10 and 20 minutes or so), unlock and remove the lid. Use a thermometer to take the temperature of the milk in the center of the pot. It should read between 179°F and 182°F.

2. Fill a large bowl or the sink with ice water, and place the inner pot in it to cool. Stir the milk occasionally, without scraping the bottom of the pot, for about 3 minutes, then take the temperature in the center of the milk. It should read between 110°F and 115°F. Remove the pot from the ice bath, dry off the outside of the pot, and place it back in the base.

3. In a small bowl, stir together the yogurt and about ½ cup of the warm milk. Add the yogurt mixture to the rest of the milk in the pot, and stir thoroughly but gently. Again, don't scrape the bottom of the pot (if there is any coagulated milk on the bottom, stirring it in can make your yogurt less smooth).

4. Secure the lid, and select Yogurt. The display should read 8:00, which indicates 8 hours of incubation time. If you prefer a longer incubation (it gets tangier the longer it's in), press the + button to increase the

time by increments of 30 minutes. When the Yogurt cycle is complete, remove the inner pot and cover it with a glass or silicone lid or place a plate on top. Refrigerate until chilled, about 4 hours, before using or stirring.

5. For Greek yogurt, line a colander or large sieve with cheesecloth. Place the colander over a large bowl. Spoon the yogurt into the colander and let it drain for 15 to 30 minutes, depending on how thick you want your yogurt.

TIP: For flavored yogurt, stir in 1 tablespoon of Mixed Berry Compote (page 84), Lemon Curd (page 85), Blueberry-Peach Sauce (page 88), or Ginger Pear Butter (page 89) per cup of yogurt.

HOMEMADE RICOTTA CHEESE

MAKES 1 CUP | PREP PLUS SITTING TIME: 20 MINUTES | YOGURT: 25 MINUTES
TOTAL TIME: 45 MINUTES, PLUS 4 HOURS TO CHILL

If you think making your own cheese at home is impossible, let me introduce you to homemade ricotta cheese in the Instant Pot. It's quick and simple, and it yields such incomparable results that store-bought will be a thing of the past. You can use it in recipes such as Ricotta Raspberry Cups (page 64) or maybe make a lasagna.

1 quart whole milk
2 to 3 tablespoons freshly squeezed
   lemon juice

⅛ teaspoon fine salt

1. Pour the milk into the Instant Pot. Select the Yogurt function, and press Adjust so that "Boil" shows in the display. Secure the lid, with the pressure valve set to the "venting" position. When the beeper sounds (between 10 and 20 minutes or so), unlock and remove the lid. Use a thermometer to take the temperature of the milk in the center of the pot. It should read between 179°F and 182°F.

2. Remove the inner pot and place it on a heatproof surface. Very gently, stir 2 tablespoons of lemon juice into the milk until the mixture starts to coagulate, about 30 to 60 seconds. You'll see the curds (white chunks of cheese) separate from the whey (thin, off-white/pale-yellow liquid). If the milk doesn't begin to coagulate, stir in 1 more tablespoon of lemon juice. Stop stirring when the milk is coagulating, and let it sit for 5 minutes.

3. Line a mesh strainer with cheesecloth or a large basket-style coffee filter, and place it over a large bowl. Pour the mixture into the strainer and let it sit for 5 to 15 minutes, or until the cheese has the consistency you like. Stir in the salt.

4. Gather up the corners of the cheesecloth and press lightly, then transfer the cheese to an airtight container and store in the refrigerator for up to 10 days.

TIP: Avoid using ultra-high-temperature (UHT) milk, which is pasteurized at extremely high temperatures.

CINNAMON-VANILLA APPLESAUCE, PAGE 87

MEASUREMENT CONVERSIONS

	US STANDARD	US STANDARD (OUNCES)	METRIC (APPROXIMATE)
VOLUME EQUIVALENTS (LIQUID)	2 tablespoons	1 fl. oz.	30 mL
	¼ cup	2 fl. oz.	60 mL
	½ cup	4 fl. oz.	120 mL
	1 cup	8 fl. oz.	240 mL
	1½ cups	12 fl. oz.	355 mL
	2 cups or 1 pint	16 fl. oz.	475 mL
	4 cups or 1 quart	32 fl. oz.	1 L
	1 gallon	128 fl. oz.	4 L
VOLUME EQUIVALENTS (DRY)	⅛ teaspoon		0.5 mL
	¼ teaspoon		1 mL
	½ teaspoon		2 mL
	¾ teaspoon		4 mL
	1 teaspoon		5 mL
	1 tablespoon		15 mL
	¼ cup		59 mL
	⅓ cup		79 mL
	½ cup		118 mL
	⅔ cup		156 mL
	¾ cup		177 mL
	1 cup		235 mL
	2 cups or 1 pint		475 mL
	3 cups		700 mL
	4 cups or 1 quart		1 L
	½ gallon		2 L
	1 gallon		4 L
WEIGHT EQUIVALENTS	½ ounce		15 g
	1 ounce		30 g
	2 ounces		60 g
	4 ounces		115 g
	8 ounces		225 g
	12 ounces		340 g
	16 ounces or 1 pound		455 g

	FAHRENHEIT (F)	CELSIUS (C) (APPROXIMATE)
OVEN TEMPERATURES	250°F	120°C
	300°F	150°C
	325°F	180°C
	375°F	190°C
	400°F	200°C
	425°F	220°C
	450°F	230°C

INDEX

ACKNOWLEDGMENTS

Sincere thanks to the team at Callisto Publishing, especially Matt Buonaguro, Rebecca Markley, Caryn Abramowitz, and Hane C. Lee. Thanks also to the contributing authors: Erica Acevedo, Srividhya Gopalakrishnan, Kristen Greazel, Lauren Keating, Barb Musick, Grace Ramirez, and Laurel Randolph.

ABOUT THE AUTHOR

JANET A. ZIMMERMAN is the author of 12 previous cookbooks, including the best-selling *Instant Pot Obsession*. An award-winning food writer and former cooking instructor, she lives and cooks in Atlanta with her partner, Dave.

CPSIA information can be obtained
at www.ICGtesting.com
Printed in the USA
JSHW010336280122
22346JS00006B/6